HAUNTED HOTELS:
TRANSITORY DANCES
WITH THE DEAD

By

Lynton Viñas

To International Readers:
This book is written in Canadian English.

HAUNTED HOTELS:
TRANSITORY DANCES WITH THE DEAD

TO:

<u>My many friends</u> who believed in me
and always saw me as the humble, simple girl
who never changed, but who grew and prospered
as a whole new world opened up for me. For all those who
stood by me, encouraged me and spent time lifting me up
and patting me on the back – thank you so much.

And, to my dear <u>Wayne</u>, whose encouragement and faith
in me has never wavered, and who puts up with
a stubborn little girl and still manages to smile.

LGV

Catalogue Number: 2017-2453601

An Education Research Associates Publication
ISBN: 978-1-928183-30-3
Distributed by

Fireside Books – Victoria, British Columbia
Part of the Peninsula Publishing Consortium

Lynton Viñas

HAUNTED HOTELS:
TRANSITORY DANCES WITH THE DEAD

TABLE OF CONTENTS

HAUNTED HOTELS:
TRANSITORY DANCES WITH THE DEAD

ABOUT THE AUTHOR

Lynton Viñas has been a manager and marketing guru for spas and beauty facilities, having worked her way up through the ranks. She is an accomplished singer and dancer who has performed at a variety of venues, and studied hotel management at the renowned International Hotel School in Cape Town, South Africa. She is from Cavite, Philippines. She is also the author of many articles on the hospitality industry and the book *Grand Hotels: Reflections on Timeless Architectural Treasures.*

HAUNTED HOTELS:
TRANSITORY DANCES WITH THE DEAD

Prologue

Things That Go Bump in the Night

I look for ghosts; but none will force

Their way to me. Is it falsely said

That there was ever intercourse

Between the living and the dead,

Alas, within here, the sceptic is fed,

And there is a creeping remorse.

Some believe there are an infinite number of universes existing side by side through which our consciousnesses constantly pass. In these universes, all possibilities exist. You are alive in some, long dead in others, and never existed in still others. Many ghosts, then, could indeed be visions of people going about their business in a parallel universe or another time or both. It is not my purpose here to profess belief or disbelief, but rather, to simply lay out some examples of hotels where strange occurrences have been reported. The reader can be the judge of the authenticity and believability.

In some parts of the world, much time is given to ghosts; in other parts, few people think about them. In the older countries, ghosts are stronger and more numerous, because the populations of those countries have kept their ghosts alive through the ages. Civilization cannot dislodge nor efface the belief in ghosts. Religion may play a role, as it emphasizes an after-life, a time when the dead will kick the lids off their coffins and rise from their graves. Yet, perhaps there are those among us, who have already left the grave and haunt the darkness that often causes us fear.

Ghosts swarm and hover all about in the tales of past, present and future. Ghosts seem to frequent certain localities more than others. Generally, the accounts of ghosts are fewer in the city than in the country, but no matter where mankind treads, dark and sinister figures are in the shadows. Of course, one should be more concerned with the sinister actions of the living, as it is they who pose the real threat.

The mind is frequently turned to morose thoughts of death, and hopefully a grand and glorious vision of an after-life for all those with religion, because we all fear the end, the darkness of eternity. This fear gives audience to shades of the dead. Belief or not is immaterial, because just as man exists, so do the ghosts in the mind. While man continues as a thinking being, ghosts will continue to exist for many, while for others they are laughable manifestations of the weak minded.

With all the ghost tales told, records kept and books written about ghosts, there seems to be no order as to the kinds and varieties of ghosts. According to philosopher, H. W. Percival, the ghost is the astral, semi-physical form that haunts a familiar location and manifests itself before those with a receptive mind.

Location is an apparent inducement to the ghost looking for a haunting ground, and old hotels are way stations in a transitory world. Hotels it seems are a natural habitat, if there indeed are wandering spirits out there. So, herein we shall explore some of the most unusual hotels where some guests have apparently lingered after death. There is an old line that was used to promote the movie about Nazi murderer, Klaus Barbie. Entitled *Hotel Terminus*, a well-known marketing genius coined the phrase: *"Hotel Terminus – where you check in but you don't check out."* Perhaps that describes many of the spirits that have been assumed to reside in some hotels. They have checked in, but are simply unable or unwilling to check out.

Since man wondered out of the primeval ocean as a fish and evolved, it is undecided whether or not there has ever been an instance of the spirit of any person appearing after death. All argument is against it; but a majority of the world's people believe in ghosts. As mentioned previously, the author is not concerned with belief or non-belief. I am merely a chronicler of

HAUNTED HOTELS:
TRANSITORY DANCES WITH THE DEAD

tales about haunted hotels, where a few people have heard things
go bump in the night.

The floor creaks from

Unseen feet, and ghosts return

Gently at twilight, gently go at dawn,

The sad intangible who grieve and yearn.

Sad men made angels of the sun, and of

The moon they made their own attendant ghosts,

Which led them back to angels after death.

HAUNTED HOTELS:
TRANSITORY DANCES WITH THE DEAD

Chapter 1

Embrace of the Dead with the Living

In the greenest of valleys

By good and bad tenanted,

Once a fair and stately hotel

Majestically reared its head,

And over all, held dominion.

It stood so proudly there!

And it served an opinion:

Something evil was left in the air.

In 1974, a not so famous writer (at the time) and his wife spent one night in Room 217 of the Stanley Hotel while on vacation during their short residency in Boulder, Colorado. Upon arrival, they discovered that they were the only overnight guests. The hotel staff was just getting ready to close for the season, and they found themselves the only guests in the place. He and his wife were served dinner in an empty dining room accompanied by canned orchestral music. Except for their own table, all the chairs were up on the tables. So the music was echoing down the hall. That night, a dream struck the author with inspiration for his next book. He dreamed of his three-year-old son running through the corridors, looking back over his shoulder, eyes wide, screaming. He was being chased by a fire-hose. The author woke up with a tremendous jerk, sweating all over, nearly falling out of bed. He sat in a chair looking out the window at the Rockies, and his furtive mind began to outline the story that would become a classic of horror. The hotel in the book is an evil entity haunted by its many victims.

In 1980, this best-selling book became a hit movie starring Jack Nicholson and Shelley Duvall. *The Shining* was a Stephen King masterpiece, based on his dream that one night in the Stanley Hotel.

The Stanley Hotel is a colonial revival hotel in Estes Park, Colorado near the entrance to the Great Rocky Mountain Park. It has panoramic views of Lake Estes and magnificent Long's Peak. It was built by Freelan Stanley of Stanley Steamer automobile fame and opened in 1909, catering to the American upper class. The hotel and its surrounding structures are listed on the National Register of Historic Places. Today, it is famous, not just as the inspiration for the scary movie, but for its history of alleged paranormal activity.

HAUNTED HOTELS:
TRANSITORY DANCES WITH THE DEAD

Freelan Oscar Stanley (1849-1940) and his twin brother Francis Edgar (1849-1918) were born in Kingfield, Maine, oddly enough, near where Stephen King lives today. In 1876, he married Flora Jane Record Tileston. Although he began his career as a teacher, in 1881 he contracted tuberculosis and resolved to adopt a more active career. From 1885 to 1904, he was co-owner with his brother at the Stanley Dry Plate Company, and they operated the Stanley Motor Carriage Company (1900-1917), earning them minor places in the early history of the automobile. F. O. Stanley was also a maker of concert-quality violins and a pioneer of reinforced concrete construction. In 1903, Freelan Stanley was stricken with a life-threatening resurgence of tuberculosis. The most highly recommended treatment of the day was fresh, dry air with lots of sunlight and a controlled diet. Therefore, like many TB sufferers of his day, Stanley resolved to take the curative air of Colorado. He and Flora arrived in Denver in March and, in June, decided to spend the rest of the summer in the mountains at Estes Park. Over the course of the season, Stanley's health improved dramatically. Impressed by the beauty of the valley and grateful for his recovery, he decided to return every year. He lived to the ripe age of 91, dying of a heart attack in 1940.

By 1907, Stanley had all but recovered and he returned to his home in Newton, Massachusetts for the winters. However, not content with the rustic accommodations, lazy pastimes and relaxed social scene of their new summer home near Denver,

Colorado, Stanley resolved to turn Estes Park into a resort town. In 1907, construction began on the Hotel Stanley, a 48-room grand hotel that catered to the upper-class scions of wealth.

The structure was completed in 1909 and featured a hydraulic elevator, dual electric and gas lighting, running water, a telephone in every guest room and a fleet of specially-designed Stanley "Model Z" Mountain Wagons to bring guests from the train depot forty kilometres away; all of this at a time when Estes Park was little more than a locale for hunters and naturalists. The hotel was not equipped with heat until 1983 and closed for the winter every year. The presence of the hotel and Stanley's own involvement greatly contributed to the growth of the Rocky Mountain National Park (established in 1915).

Stanley operated the hotel almost as a pastime, remarking once that he spent more money than he made each summer. In 1926, he sold the Stanley to a private company incorporated for the sole purpose of running it. The venture failed and, in 1929, Stanley purchased his property out of foreclosure selling it again to fellow auto and hotel magnate, Roe Emery. During Emery's tenure as owner, the structures were painted white inside and out and most of the original electro-gas fixtures were replaced.

Now, as for paranormal activity, the book and movie have been very good for business, so good that the original, uncut version of the film is shown nightly at the hotel. However, that is not the only scary thing at the hotel.

HAUNTED HOTELS:
TRANSITORY DANCES WITH THE DEAD

Today, there are 140 rooms at the hotel, and each one holds a mystery. Over the years, there have been many strange happenings here. In fact, the original owner, Freelan Stanley and his wife, whose pictures hang in the hotel lobby, have often been seen about the hotel. Stanley and his wife, apparently prefer to haunt separately, as Mr. Stanley appears at the bar, while Mrs. Stanley can sometimes be heard happily playing the piano. They are not alone, as many other sightings have occurred throughout the hotel's history. The land's previous owner, the 4th Earl of Dunraven, haunts Room 407. He is occasionally seen in the room, standing in the corner, the smell of pipe tobacco lingering in the air. Ghostly children haunt Room 418. Sounds of laughter and running footsteps can sometimes be heard in the room and throughout the hotel's hallways. Strangest of all are the indentations on the bed despite no one having been in the room. Another woman claims to have been talking on the phone and suddenly feeling someone touching her leg, the hands being small, as if they were a child's. According to the Stanley Hotel's official website, the Concert Hall is also haunted, and sometimes, if Mrs. Stanley is playing the piano and someone opens the door a loud "get out" shout reverberates all about. A ghost that calls herself Lucy has sometimes conversed with guests in the concert hall, but as the guests turn to leave and look back, she has disappeared. She can be heard humming mournful melodies in the night.

HAUNTED HOTELS:
TRANSITORY DANCES WITH THE DEAD

The room of primary interest is the one where Stephen King slept – number 217. Although he only had a horrible nightmare there, the room has a certain aura to it that even King admits to having felt. One night in 1911, a thunderstorm knocked out the hotel's power, and chambermaid Elizabeth Wilson entered Room 217 with a lit candle to relight the gas lamps. What she didn't know was that the room was already filled with leaking gas, and as soon as she entered, it literally exploded. She did not die but was badly burned. Some people have claimed that a chambermaid has come into the room and said to them "be careful," then turns and leaves. She is obviously not a present employee as she is always wearing a maid's uniform from the early 1900's. Another frequent uninvited interloper is a man named Paul who worked at the hotel, and as security staff would often enforce the 11:00 PM curfew on noisiness. Sometimes people who are being a bit loud after 11 have said they have been gently touched, but there is no one there, but a voice can be heard softly uttering, "quiet please."

For years, a foul odour would sometimes accompany people down the hallways. They would complain about the stink for awhile, but after a few hours, they begin to say they smelled a pleasant odour. It is surmised that the ghost, referred to as Stinky Eddie, takes umbrage to the moniker and simply changes his smell. He is a bit of a lady's man, frequently kissing women on their cheeks when it is dark. The kiss is not seen, just felt.

HAUNTED HOTELS:
TRANSITORY DANCES WITH THE DEAD

A myriad of strange phenomena have occurred over the years like sounds of parties in the dining room after it has closed. Even sceptics, who have investigated, claim to have heard thumping, saw strange lights, shadows and orbs floating about. Some have had glasses shattered or objects seem to move about.

One of the more recent occurrences was in April of 2016, when a guest photographed the stairwell and captured a ghostly image on his camera. So far, no one has been able to explain the ghostly image.

Photo taken in 2016 by a guest.

Probably the most intense chill is when one strolls alone down the corridors of the hotel. There is a certain trepidation that seems to overwhelm the individual with an intense desire to get to one's room and slam the door to hopefully lock out whatever entity might be lurking about outside just waiting with steely cold arms longing to enjoy the embrace of the dead with the living.

HAUNTED HOTELS:
TRANSITORY DANCES WITH THE DEAD

*A night time arrival is suggested for those who want
the full eerie effect of this ghostly haunt.*

Lynton Viñas

Chapter 2

Horror of Horrors

Take this kiss upon the brow!

And, in parting from you now,

This much let me avow

You are not wrong, who deem

That my days have been a dream;

Yet if hope has flown away

In a night, or in a day,

In a vision, or in none,

Is it therefore the less gone?

All that we see or seem

Is but a dream within a dream.

In Kent, England there is a quaint, tiny, picturesque village called Rye, and there sits within it environs a six hundred year old stately hotel called Mermaid Inn, and within its walls are rumoured to be spirits that simply will not rest after all these years.

The Mermaid Inn is an integral part of Rye social life today, and was also the same in the past. It was established in the 12th century and has a long, turbulent, sometimes extremely violent history. The current building dates from 1420 and has 16th-century additions in the English Tudor style, but cellars built in 1156 still survive and are being used today. The inn has a strong connection with the Hawkhurst Gang, who were notorious smugglers and cutthroats in the 1730's and 1740's. They frequented The Mermaid Inn, where they would sit with their weapons on the tables prepared to do battle with anyone who dared challenge them. Some of the smugglers, their mistresses and other characters are apparently the most frequent haunters of this inn today.

The inglorious history of the inn continued into the 1800's as it passed though several owners. The inn functioned as a club in the early 1900's, after it was owned by May Aldington, mother of the novelist Richard Aldington. It was then a popular locale for many artists, including Dame Ellen Terry, Lord Alfred Douglas (Oscar Wilde's "Bosie"), A.C. and E. F. Benson and Rupert Brooke. In 1945, during World War II, the inn functioned as a garrison for Canadian officers. It was later purchased by a Canadian, who had been stationed there.

It seems that the ghosts here prefer to haunt individual rooms rather than the inn as a whole. Some rooms have become famous for their uninvited guests. Approximately one in five rooms has reported strange occurrences.

1. Room 1 is said to be haunted by a lady in white or grey who sits in the chair by the fireplace. Guests have reported waking up in the morning and finding their clothes on the chair wet, despite no windows or pipe work being near the chair. The lady will often look directly at people with a horrid expression and then gradually fade away.

2. Room 10 is said to be haunted by the ghost of a man who has terrified guests by walking through the bathroom wall into the main room.

3. Room 16 was said to be the scene of a duel involving two men. This occurred in the 1600's. After fighting through some of the nearby rooms, one of the men was killed, dragged into the adjacent room and thrown through a trapdoor into the dungeon below. Many unexplained light anomalies have been recorded in the middle of the night. On one occasion an employee was tending to the fireplace when all of the bottles on the shelf at the other end of the room fell off; the experience caused him to resign.

4. Room 17 is supposedly haunted by the ghost of a woman who was the wife of the Hawkhurst gang founder George Gray. She apparently does not materialize, but many guests have awakened in the night and see the chair rocking on its own, and found the room icy cold. Several guests have heard a quiet voice saying, "where be my husband, George Gray?"

5. Room 19 is said to be haunted by a gentleman in old-fashioned clothes. One American guest reported seeing him sitting at the end of her bed. She was so frightened she ran to her friend's adjacent room and refused to stay another night at the inn.

As alluded to earlier, there seems to be a penchant among the ghosts here to only concentrate on individual rooms to haunt; however, on occasion, the ghost of a former maid, who was a girlfriend of one of the Hawkhurst gang and was killed by a gang member for fear she knew too much and would expose them, has been seen in the lobby.

Room 19, where a man likes to gaze down

upon sleeping women. Apparently even ghosts can be perverts.

Due to its haunted reputation, the inn has been featured on many paranormal television shows. Judith Blincow, who owned the inn when this book went to press and has worked there since 1980, states, "Although I have not personally seen ghosts, I certainly have met some very convinced and frightened guests who believe they have seen them. Still, it does not appear to have hurt our business at all."

An elderly French woman who watched a rocking chair move back and forth with no one sitting in it, said, "I know there was something sitting there. I couldn't see it, but I could feel it."

One night a woman lay down exhausted from a day of sightseeing. She closed her eyes, and as she did a cold, icy hand touched her lower leg and was slowly edging its way upward. She screamed, reared upright, and there at the foot of the bed was a man staring longingly at her. Horror of horrors, it was her husband!

Chapter 3

Hollywood Ghostly Hotel Mayhem

Ghostly things moan in sorrow.

Assailed they a grand acting state,

And round about was great glory,

That never blushed and always bloomed.

Alas, it is a dim-remembered story

The spectre now in a hotel entombed.

Los Angeles is promoted as a land of fairy tales where the lowly waitress gets discovered and becomes an instant star. Unfortunately, this is indeed a very grand illusion, because like everything else in America, where the oligarchy of privilege rules with impunity, those born into the close-knit Hollywood community of producers, directors and stars have an inside track to stardom simply because of who their parents were. Doors rarely swing wide open for the poorly-connected.

HAUNTED HOTELS:
TRANSITORY DANCES WITH THE DEAD

Perhaps this inbreeding accounts for the low quality of product that is ground out by the second and third generations of actors, actress, directors and producers. However, there was a time when the lightning of fame struck and the poor farm boy from Nebraska could be plucked from obscurity into the top echelon of great stars. So, if you are going to be a ghost, why not haunt some Los Angeles hotel, rather than return to the farm in Nebraska to haunt the cornfields.

The list of ghosts, famous and not famous, some even infamous, is long and varied, so let's take a journey through the La La Land of spectres that inhabit some hotels in the Los Angeles area.

Cecil Hotel (Renamed Stay on Main)

This was home to one of the most infamous killers of all time. A quote from author, Wayne Fryc, sums up this formerly run-down, skid row hotel: "This is a place every bit as sinister as the Overlook Hotel of *Shining* fame. There is no crazed, wild-eyed, dishevelled Jack Nicholson lurking about, but just knowing that the infamous Night Stalker roamed the halls, sit in the lobby, slept on the 14th floor, and, no doubt, planned some of his murders here sends shivers up and down your spine. There is a foreboding feeling of dread that seems to grip you when you walk into the lobby. This is not in and of itself an inherently evil place, but there is a chill to it knowing that the walls harbour knowledge of two prolific killers who embraced the dark side."

HAUNTED HOTELS:
TRANSITORY DANCES WITH THE DEAD

The Cecil was constructed in 1924 by hotelier, William Banks Hanner. Built in the Art Deco style, the hotel cost $1,000,000 (a princely sum at the time). It had an opulent marble lobby with stained glass windows, potted palms and alabaster statuary. Hanner had invested confidently in the enterprise, but within five years of its opening, the United States sank into the Great Depression. The road on which the hotel stood, Main Street, quickly declined into the area known as Skid Row, with as many as 10,000 homeless people living nearby, and by 1950, it had become a hotel catering to the down and out in a society that is notorious for its cavalier attitude about poverty. Its reputation for attracting a criminal element also grew. It was refurbished in 2007 and re-branded the *Stay on Main* in 2011. However, the upgrade has had little effect on quieting the restless spirits that seem to still roam about.

For many years, one of the most popular web-sites featured a camera on the rooftop of a nearby building that was focused on the front of the hotel, where all kinds of nefarious activities took place. Apparently, it has been removed, as the new owners found it unseemly to promote the negative aspects of the hotel.

The hotel was sold to hotelier, Richard Born, for $30 million in 2014, and another New-York based firm, Simon Baron Development, acquired a 99 year ground lease on the property. In November 2016, it was reported that the Cecil Hotel could receive special recognition from the city of Los Angeles after the

HAUNTED HOTELS:
TRANSITORY DANCES WITH THE DEAD

Cultural Heritage Commission voted unanimously to consider the downtown structure as a historic-cultural monument. I am sure the ghosts could care less about the designation.

A review of the notorious occurrences follows below:

In 2013, the Cecil Hotel (*Stay on Main*) became the focus of a viral internet video, which showed surveillance footage of the bizarre behaviour of a young Canadian student, Elisa Lam, in one of the hotel's elevators. On 19 February, her naked body was found inside one of the water supply tanks on the hotel roof. Lam had gone missing almost three weeks earlier on January 31, 2013, and her decomposed body was discovered in one of the rooftop water tanks by a maintenance worker after guests had complained about low water pressure and water that tasted funny. Authorities later ruled Lam's death as an accidental drowning. Video surveillance footage taken from inside an elevator shortly before her disappearance showed Lam acting strangely, pressing multiple elevator buttons, hiding in the corner of the elevator, and waving her arms wildly, causing widespread speculation about the cause of her death. After the elevator video went public, many started to believe in a more paranormal explanation, some suggesting Lam was possessed by an unknown entity. Lam was thought to have a bipolar disorder, which could have contributed to her death as well as her strange behaviour. The same day she disappeared, another guest had complained about a dark shadow in the elevator.

HAUNTED HOTELS:
TRANSITORY DANCES WITH THE DEAD

The aforementioned video is 4 minutes long, and it creates more questions than it answers. It begins with Lam casually dressed in a red hoodie, black shorts and sandals, walking into the elevator car on the 14th floor. She crouches down inside to look at the numbers on the buttons, presses one, and steps back into the back right corner of the car, waiting for it to move. Before the door closes, she looks out into the hall with a concerned countenance. A few seconds pass, and still the door doesn't close. Lam steps forward and cautiously leans toward the open door. She looks out into the hall, first to the right, then to the left. Then, she frantically jumps back into the elevator. Whatever she saw, or heard, seems to have frightened her, and she appears to be shivering and trying to hide in the front right corner, where it would be harder for anyone walking by to see her. She does not hide there for long until she looks out again, this time staring down the hall to the right for 10 seconds, at which point her behaviour becomes highly erratic.

Lam steps out of the car, then in, then back out, and then disappears from the frame as she is obviously in the hall to the left of the open door. Her right arm dangles into view a few times as if she is motioning with it, so it is clear she is standing just to the left of the open door, where she stands for awhile, at which point she re-enters the elevator with her hands raised in an almost defensive manner, and then she frantically pushes numerous buttons, obviously trying to get the door to close. When the door doesn't close, Lam steps into the hall again and begins the most disturbing action of all. She stares intently to the right of the frame up the hallway, and begins to wave her hands as if gesturing for someone to stop. She waves her arms with wrists limp and then wrings her hands. She appears to be almost begging someone not to come toward her. However, no one can be seen as she takes a few stuttering steps while the elevator closes. As it does, there seems to be a quick flash of what is a dark shadow in the hallway. The other ironical element is that she exits to the left, and to the left there is a mirrored wall. Why did she not go to the right down the hallway? That was the last that was seen of her until her body was found.

Bank of Cecil Hotel elevators on 14th floor - notice that if you exit left there is a mirrored wall. Why did she not go right and down the hallway?

The story did not end here, though. It became an overnight sensation as the hotel's past began to suggest paranormal sinister elements might be at play, even having caused some guests to commit suicide over the years due to subconscious mind manipulation by unknown entities.

This particular incident led to a deeper interest in the hotel's past by investigative reporters and paranormal researchers, which revealed a prolific history of suicide, murder or unexplained deaths at the hotel almost since it first opened. The Cecil seems to be disproportionately blighted by tragedy and violence when compared to most hotels.

One of the hotel's most interesting guests was the famous Black Dalia. The Black Dahlia was a nickname given to Elizabeth Short (July 29, 1924 – January 15, 1947), an American woman who was the victim of a much-publicized murder in 1947. Short acquired the moniker posthumously from newspapers in the habit of nicknaming crimes they found particularly lurid. The Black Dahlia nickname may have been derived from a film noir murder mystery, *The Blue Dahlia*, released in April 1946. Short was found mutilated; her body sliced in half at the waist, on January 15, 1947 in Leimert Park, Los Angeles. Short's unsolved murder has been the source of widespread speculation, leading to many suspects, along with several books, television and film adaptations of the story. Short's murder is one of the oldest unsolved murder cases in Los Angeles history.

HAUNTED HOTELS:
TRANSITORY DANCES WITH THE DEAD

Elizabeth Short – The Black Dahlia

Short made the Cecil her last stop before her death in 1947, though this is disputed by some. The registry has been lost, but meticulous research seems to indicate she spent the night before her murder there.

On 19 November 1931, the Los Angeles Times reported that a search for 46 year-old Manhattan Beach resident W.K Norton was over. He had checked into the Cecil as "James Willys of Chicago" a week earlier and, once in his room, had taken a number of poison capsules. This appears to be the earliest known suicide at the hotel.

Less than a year later, the Los Angeles Times reported another suicide at the hotel: Benjamin Dodich, 25, had shot himself in the head in his room and his body was found the next morning by a maid. There was no suicide note.

In late July 1934, a 53 year-old former Army Medical Corps sergeant named Louis D. Borden slashed his throat with a razor in his room. Borden left a note mentioning his ill health. There was some suspicion it was not a suicide, as the method used was highly unusual. The case remains open.

HAUNTED HOTELS:
TRANSITORY DANCES WITH THE DEAD

In March of 1937, it was reported that Grace E. Magro had fallen from a ninth story window. Police were unsure as to whether this had been an accident or suicide, and her fall had been broken by suspended telephone wiring which was entangled about her body.

In January 1938, Roy Thompson, a 35 year-old marine fireman took a leap from the hotel's top floor. He had been registered there for several weeks and his body was found on the skylight of a building next door.

In May of 1939, a thin, almost emaciated looking sailor, Erwin C. Neblett, 39, of the USS Wright, died in his room after taking poison, and in January of the following year it was reported that teacher, Dorothy Sceiger, 45, had employed the same method in the exact same room.

In September 1944, Dorothy Jean Purcell, 19, threw her newborn son from a window. Apparently unaware she was pregnant, Purcell had not wanted to wake her sleeping partner, shoe salesman, Ben Levine, when she woke with stomach pains. So she went to the nearby rest room and delivered the baby herself. Believing the child to be dead, she threw it from a window and the tiny body was later found on the roof of an adjacent building. She was charged with homicide. However, she was found not guilty by reason of insanity.

In November 1947, 35 year-old Robert Smith of Long Beach met his death after falling from the Cecil's seventh floor. The window that had to be raised to jump out apparently had no finger prints on it. Still, it was ruled a suicide.

On October 22, 1954, Helen Gurnee stepped from her window, also on the seventh floor, and landed on top of the hotel's marquee.

On February 11 of 1962, Julia Frances Moore, 50, climbed out of her eighth floor room window, jumped and landed in a second story interior light well. She left no note, just a bus ticket and 59 cents in change on the nightstand.

On October 12, 1962, Pauline Otton, 27, had been arguing with her estranged husband Dewey in a room on the ninth floor when he decided he was going out to get some dinner. In his absence, she decided she had enough also and jumped out the window, landing on top of a pedestrian, George Gianinni, 65. Both were killed instantly. Since no one saw Pauline jump, police initially thought that there had been a double suicide, but on closer examination, it was found that George had his hands in his pockets, which would have been unlikely if he had jumped. Oh, and there were no finger prints found on the window.

On June 4, 1964, Goldie Osgood, a retired telephone operator, was found dead in her ransacked room by a hotel worker distributing phone books. Osgood had been stabbed, strangled and raped. Soon after, Jacques B. Ehlinger, 29, was seen walking through Pershing Square in bloodstained clothing. He was arrested, but cleared of the crime, as the blood was found to be a different type than the victim. He simply said that he had been in a fight. The case remains open.

It appears that there have been at least fifteen deaths at the Cecil, resulting from non-natural causes: either as a result of suicide, accident or murder. With over 700 rooms, maybe this is not extraordinary, but this is not where the weird nature of this hotel ends. There was one resident who brought so much terror to Los Angeles and surrounding areas with his methodically sadistic stalking of prey that he was called "the night stalker."

Richard Ramirez (1960-2013), an American serial killer, rapist and burglar lived at the hotel in 1984 - 1985. He was convicted of 14 murders, but suspected of many more. He lived on the Cecil's 14th floor in a $14-a-night room. Yes, it is the same floor on which Elisa Lam would also stay many years later and create a sensation with her elevator antics and death.

Ramirez's highly publicized crime spree terrorized the residents of the greater Los Angeles area, and later the residents of the San Francisco Bay area from June 1984 until August 1985. An avowed Satanist, he never expressed any remorse for his crimes, famously saying as he was sentenced to death, "I'll see you at Disneyland."

An admirer of Ramirez was Johann Unteweger (1950-1994) who was an Austrian serial killer. Convicted of murder in 1974 in Austria, he was released in 1990 and proclaimed a grand example of rehabilitation.

HAUNTED HOTELS:
TRANSITORY DANCES WITH THE DEAD

Unteweger became a journalist and a renowned celebrity. Upon his release, his autobiography *Fegefeuer oder die Reise ins Zuchthaus* was taught in schools and his stories for children were performed on the radio. Unterweger hosted television programs which discussed criminal rehabilitation, and he reported as a journalist for the public broadcaster, including reporting stories concerning seven murders for which he was later found guilty. Deep within his psyche, he harboured admiration for the Night Stalker and in 1991 he was hired by an Austrian magazine to write about crime in Los Angeles. Where else would he stay while in Los Angeles but the Cecil Hotel, the very place where his hero, Richard Ramirez, stayed? While there, he murdered three prostitutes, strangling them with their own bras. Unterweger met with local police, even going so far as to participate in a ride-along of the city's red light districts. The police were impressed with his knowledge of criminal investigation.

After returning to Austria, he was sought for the crimes when Los Angeles police found evidence connecting him to the murdered prostitutes, but by that time he had been captured in Miami and extradited to Austria where he was standing trial for the murder of 11 women. He was swiftly convicted, but before he could be extradited to also stand trial in the USA, he hanged himself. Like Ramirez and Lam, he stayed on the 14th floor, and it is on this floor that some guests have reported strange occurrences, including seeing mysterious shadows flittering in an unusual manner about the hallway. The floating ghost of a boy has been seen staring through a fourth floor window, but that is only one of many encounters that have occurred over the years. Apparently, the 14th floor is the most haunted with more reports of strange sounds and dark shadows occurring than on any other floor. There was one report of a person having a conversation with a lady in the 14th floor lobby, but after awhile she seemed to simply vaporize and disappear into thin air. Another guest reported meeting a prostitute in the elevator, whom he asked to his room. They went to the 14th floor, where he waited patiently for her to come out of the bathroom. She never came out, and when he opened the bathroom door it was empty. Oh, the women went by the name Shannon. One of the prostitutes murdered by Unterweger was named Shannon Exley.

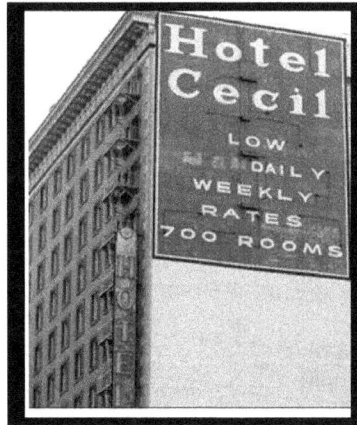

Although the name has been changed, you cannot change the eeriness, the feeling of something unusual and foreboding. Still, there is a pull, a strange attraction that lures and entices.

HAUNTED HOTELS:
TRANSITORY DANCES WITH THE DEAD

Author, Wayne Frye, while living in Los Angeles, was fascinated by the place and spent many hours just studying the webcam that was once on a rooftop across from the hotel. He said in a Los Angles newspaper artricle, "There is a mystique to the hotel. As you watch the array of people passing by, you see a microcosm of a society where people are discarded like worn out products. These are people on the edge of a precipice of despair. They long for a hand up, but America is not a society which very willingly offers compassion. The rough individualism that is preached has gobbled up most of these individuals and they are complacently waiting for the end. Going into the hotel are people with stooped shoulders that seemed to be bearing the burdens of lost hope, weighted down with desperation of the spirit. Yet, there are still those with a glimmer of hope in their eyes, a belief that this is only a way station on the road to rcncwal. Watching this hotel makes you realize it is a monument to those poor souls who passed through here on their way to oblivion or on their way to the high road of hope."

Chateau Marmont - Los Angeles

Converted to a hotel in the 1930s, the Chateau Marmot is an exclusive and elegant hotel off the Sunset Strip known as a discreet hideaway for celebrities. For some, it has been the setting for meltdowns, affairs and drunken adventures. From Britney Spears to Jim Morrison, it has been a place where the glare of the spotlight seems to dim and some anonymity can be found.

HAUNTED HOTELS:
TRANSITORY DANCES WITH THE DEAD

Notorious partier, John Belushi, apparently liked the place so much his ghost now resides there as Bungalow 3, where he fatally overdosed in 1982, is the site of strange occurrences. The most disturbing story involves a toddler whose family stayed there in 1999 and his parents would hear him laughing alone. They asked him why he was laughing and he replied, "The man is so funny." Later, as his mother was looking through a book of celebrity guests, the little boy pointed to a picture of Belushi and said, "The funny man." Now, I have seen the movie *Animal House* and clips from when Belushi was on *Saturday Night Live*, and my personal tastes do not go toward his gross form of humour, but then again, I have just never found sticking asparagus up your nose and snorting like a pig particularly funny. Apparently, the toddler thought it was hilarious.

In 1926, Fred Horowitz, a prominent Los Angeles attorney, chose the site at Marmont Lane and Sunset Boulevard to construct an apartment building. Horowitz had recently traveled to Europe for inspiration and returned to California with photos of a Gothic Chateau along the Loire River. Horowitz commissioned his brother-in-law, European-trained architect Arnold A. Weitzman to design the seven-story, L-shaped building.

In 1929, Chateau Marmont opened its doors to the public as the newest residence in Hollywood. Due to the high rents and inability to keep tenants for long-term commitments during the depression, Horowitz chose to sell the apartment building to Albert E. Smith for $750,000. In 1931, Chateau Marmont was converted into a hotel. The apartments became suites with kitchens and living rooms. The property was also refurbished with antiques from depression-era estate sales.

Designed and constructed to be earthquake proof, Chateau Marmont survived major earthquakes in 1933, 1953, 1971, 1987 and 1994 without sustaining any major structural damage. Nine Spanish cottages, as well as a swimming pool, were built next to the hotel in the 1930's and were acquired by the hotel in the 1940's.

It has been a recognizable structure in many movies over the years, one of the most famous being Oliver Stone's classic, *The Doors*. It has also figured prominently in many television shows and been alluded to in several songs by famous artists. The actress, Sharon Tate, who was murdered by the Manson family, stayed here for a short time with her husband, director, Roman Polanski, in 1968 just before they moved into the home where she was murdered. Jim Morrison, of the aforementioned *Doors* rock band, was here in 1970 a short time before his demise. Other famous guests have been Billy Wilder, Hunter S. Thompson, Annie Leibovitz, Dorothy Parker, Bruce Weber, F. Scott Fitzgerald, Tim Burton, Jay McInerney, Terry Richardson, Death Grips and Ville Valo. Author, Wayne Frye, on his visit here said, "I don't believe in ghosts, but I slept with the light on."

HAUNTED HOTELS:
TRANSITORY DANCES WITH THE DEAD

Perhaps the scariest actor of all time, Boris Karloff, who played the original *Frankenstein* in 1932, lived here a number of years. The suite in which he resided has produced a number of scary encounters. Several guests have awakened to see a woman hovering over their beds. Perhaps the culprit is Elsa Lanchester, who played the title role alongside Karloff in the *Bride of Frankenstein* and was married to none other than Charles Laughton, the original Hunchback of Notre Dame. Other guests have reported seeing strange shadows in various places among the bungalows and hallways.

The popular song by the rock group Eagles, *Hotel California*, is based on the Marmont, where they stayed during an engagement, and may well have had some unusual encounters as related in the song:

On a dark desert highway, cool wind in my hair
Warm smell of colitas, rising up through the air
Up ahead in the distance, I saw a shimmering light
My head grew heavy and my sight grew dim
I had to stop for the night
There she stood in the doorway;
I heard the mission bell
And I was thinking to myself,
"This could be Heaven or this could be Hell"
Then she lit up a candle and she showed me the way
There were voices down the corridor,

HAUNTED HOTELS:
TRANSITORY DANCES WITH THE DEAD

I thought I heard them say...

Welcome to the Hotel California

Such a lovely place (Such a lovely place)

Such a lovely face

Plenty of room at the Hotel California

Any time of year (Any time of year)

You can find it here

Her mind is Tiffany-twisted, she got the Mercedes bends

She got a lot of pretty, pretty boys she calls friends

How they dance in the courtyard, sweet summer sweat.

Some dance to remember, some dance to forget

So I called up the Captain,

"Please bring me my wine"

He said, "Haven't had that spirit here since nineteen sixty nine"

And still those voices are calling from far away,

Wake you up in the middle of the night

Just to hear them say...

Welcome to the Hotel California

Such a lovely place (Such a lovely place)

Such a lovely face

They livin' it up at the Hotel California

What a nice surprise (what a nice surprise)

Lynton Viñas

HAUNTED HOTELS:
TRANSITORY DANCES WITH THE DEAD

Bring your alibis

Mirrors on the ceiling,

The pink champagne on ice

And she said "We are all just prisoners here of our own device"

And in the master's chambers,

They gathered for the feast

They stab it with their steely knives,

But they just can't kill the beast

Last thing I remember, I was

Running for the door

I had to find the passage back

To the place I was before

"Relax," said the night man,

"We are programmed to receive.

You can check-out any time you like,

But you can never leave!"

(© 1977 Don Felder, Don Henley, Glenn Frey)

Although the lyrics are said by the band to be an indictment of American culture, one cannot help but sincerely postulate on what effect the Marmont had on the formulation of the song. The last three lines are particularly relevant to the mysteries of the Marmont:

"We are programmed to receive.

You can check-out any time you like,

HAUNTED HOTELS:
TRANSITORY DANCES WITH THE DEAD

But you can never leave!"

John Belushi can attest to checking out, but only in a body bag, and according to some, like the song, he has never left the Marmont. So, if you decide to check into the Marmont, you may check out, but one day find out you have never left – interpret that!

The hotel stands grand and majestic as you approach from Hollywood. Below is the bungalow where John Belushi met his demise, and where his ghost supposedly spends most of its time.

Lynton Viñas

HAUNTED HOTELS:
TRANSITORY DANCES WITH THE DEAD

The Hollywood Roosevelt Hotel

How would you like to hob-knob with Marilyn Monroe? Well, fortunately, the Hollywood Roosevelt is making a glamorous comeback after extensive renovations, and if you want to see Marilyn, there is a good chance she might drop by her old room – 1200. In fact, among the Hollywood star ghosts, she is probably one of the most prolific. She lived here as her fame grew, even filming here on occasion. It seems that she is most often seen in the mirrors in the room, looking back at the guests with a quizzical expression, almost saying, "What are you doing in my room?" Over the years, her appearances have diminished somewhat, maybe being eternally young as a ghost, perhaps she is frightened at the thought of being around so many old people who now frequent the hotel in Hollywood.

"I am good, but not an angel.
I do sin, but I am not the devil.
I am just a small girl in a big world trying to find someone to love."
Marilyn Monroe

One mirror from the room, after Monroe's death, was moved to the manager's office. A person dusting the mirror was shocked at seeing a reflection in it of a beautiful blond sad lady standing behind her. She turned and the lady was gone. Turning back to the mirror, the lady was staring from inside the mirror at her, but slowly dissipated. Later, when looking at a picture of Marilyn Monroe that hung on the lobby wall, she immediately recognized her as the lady in the mirror. Today, this mirror hangs in the lobby next the elevators, and most employees avoid looking into it, but many guests have reported seeing a beautiful blond woman's reflection. A cardboard cut-out of Monroe is conveniently placed across from the mirror, but sometimes the night shift will find it turned over onto the floor.

HAUNTED HOTELS:
TRANSITORY DANCES WITH THE DEAD

1950's heartthrob, Montgomery Clift, who spent 3 months here apparently liked the hotel so much that he returned after his death. Maids often feel like they are being watched when they clean room 928, where he stayed. He has been seen pacing the hallway, and one female guest awoke, thinking her husband had gotten out of bed and was sitting in a chair near the window. She was shocked when she felt a hand reach over and caress her. It was her husband, but who was that in the chair? She looked back at the chair and the man was gone. He reportedly taps many guests on their shoulders, but never speaks. He always played the shy silent type, so perhaps that is understandable.

The ghost of Carol Lombard prefers the upper floors, where she is often seen wandering the hallways. In the Blossom Room downstairs there is a spot that is always 10 degrees cooler than the rest of the room. This is where the first Oscar ceremonies were held, and some people have also seen two men, one in a black tux and one in a white suit, circa 1930's style clothing, often materialize and seem to walk out into the lobby to simply disappear from view. At least they are well dressed in case they get an invitation to a formal party.

It was reported that in 1975 a woman sat in the lobby talking to a very handsome man. The man had a pencil thin moustache, and was met by a beautiful woman. They walked to the elevator and went up to the Penthouse suite. She looked at a picture on the lobby wall of Clark Gable and Carol Lombard. It just so happens they usually stayed in the Penthouse suite. She immediately recognized the couple she saw as Lombard and Gable.

Not all of ghosts here are grownups. A little girl named Caroline and her brother reportedly drowned in the pool while their father was out running errands; since then, she has been spotted or heard around the hotel. She likes to call up people from the house phone in the lobby and she and her brother can be heard, but not seen, playing around the Jacuzzi. However, they do apparently leave wet footprints.

This is one of the most haunted places in all of Los Angeles. Hey, maybe an enterprising director could hang out here and cast all these old ghost stars in a movie together. If their egos did not get in the way, it could be a real "thriller."

HAUNTED HOTELS:
TRANSITORY DANCES WITH THE DEAD

<u>Knickerbocker Hotel - Hollywood</u>

Marilyn Monroe was someone who loved a good time, which may account for the fact she is not happy haunting just one hotel, because she also apparently loves to visit the Knickerbocker as a ghostly apparition. For some reason, her favourite haunt here is the washroom next to the bar, which used to be known as the Lido Room. This was where she would go with her beau at the time, Hall of Fame baseball player, Joe DiMaggio. In fact, in 1954, they spent their honeymoon at the Knickerbocker.

Today, this place is an apartment building for senior citizens, but when it was converted, apparently the ghosts preferred to stick around and entertain the oldsters. The oldest ghost is apparently that of famed silent movie star Rudolph Valentino, who has been plying his ghostly trade here since the 1920's. The hotel opened four years before the soon-to-be Great Depression – 1925. It was an apartment building for the affluent. The only problem was that within 4 years many of the affluent (or formally affluent) were jumping out of buildings everywhere over the despair of losing all they had in the great stock market crash of 1929. Still, while the country was in the throes of the depression, Hollywood was turning out some of its finest work, as people desperately needed entertainment to get their minds off the miseries caused by the boom and bust cycle that is at the very heart of the capitalist system which chews up men and women to feed the frenzied engine of greed.

HAUNTED HOTELS:
TRANSITORY DANCES WITH THE DEAD

Workers in the basement have told tales of shadows flittering about. One shadow often seems to slowly materialize and based on descriptions, it appeared to be the famous MGM dress designer, Irene Gibbons, who took a dive off the rooftop back in 1962. Once, a worker claimed that Irene asked him how she could get out of the hotel as she was trapped in the basement. He turned and pointed toward the door, but when he turned back, she was gone.

HAUNTED HOTELS:
TRANSITORY DANCES WITH THE DEAD

The guests here read like a who's who of past stars. Elvis loved staying here, and some people claim to have heard him singing in the room where he used to stay.

The tales of undulating, quivering shadows abound throughout the hotel as well as doors closing and opening seemingly on their own. Are there unseen hands causing this mischief? The mirrors in some rooms, when it was hotel, would suddenly mist up and outlines in the shape of a woman or a man mysteriously began to form.

HAUNTED HOTELS:
TRANSITORY DANCES WITH THE DEAD

Perhaps the ghost which exhibits the most suaveness and penchant for being polite is none other than silent screen star, Rudolph Valentino, who died in 1926 at the age of 31. He loved hanging out in the bar and enjoyed an occasional tango with women there. His English was not that good, so it was probably fortunate the Italian native was around at the time of silent films. His silence apparently did not transfer to the nether world of ghosts, as some women (no men have sighted him) have reported seeing a distinguished-looking, dashingly handsome man pass them in the lobby as they were on the way to the bar. He smiles, nods his head and says, "Good evening ma'am" with a heavy Italian accent. They are so overwhelmed by him that they get short of breath, stop, turn and look to see where he is going. However, he has disappeared. Bewildered, they continue to the bar, where they see a picture on the wall. Alas, it is the man they passed. The caption under the picture reads, Rudolph Valentino.

Famous magician, Harry Houdini, always wanted to come back from the dead, because of a fascination with the occult and his choice of arrival from the great beyond – the Knickerbocker. He and his wife made a deal that if he died before she did, he would try to contact her after his death. So, on Halloween of 1926, (the first anniversary of his death) Houdini's wife conducted a séance on the roof of the Knickerbocker. When Houdini failed to put in an appearance, she continued holding annual séances at the hotel for over a decade, obviously, without success. However, it

Lynton Viñas

HAUNTED HOTELS:
TRANSITORY DANCES WITH THE DEAD

aapears that some others have apparently made it back here from the great beyond. There is a society which still holds these séances today. It has been a long and patient wait for Harry, but perhaps he has been busy entertaining the angels with magic shows all these years, or perhaps he is with the devil putting on shows for tormented souls in hell.

The beautiful mentally ill actress, Frances Farmer, lived at the hotel for many years, drinking herself into the dark oblivion of insanity. In 1943, police knocked on her door. They had a warrant for unpaid DUI fines in hand. They eventually opened the door with a passkey, where they found Farmer naked and writhing like a wild animal with rabies on the floor. She refused to cooperate with the police, screaming, kicking and hollering at them. Eventually, she was carried through the hotel kicking, spitting and screaming. One onlooker called it an academy award performance. For many years, Farmer battled mental illness and she died in 1970. Her ghost apparently has only visited here twice, with two people who stayed in the room where she was arrested saying they were awakened in the night by the obscene screaming of a woman. They turned on the lights and no one was there.

Deaths of the famous have been a regular occurrence here. Famed director of *Birth of a Nation* (1915) and *Intolerance* (1916), D.W. Griffith had a heart attack under what is now known as the D.W. Griffith chandelier. The chandelier was the finest of its kind anywhere in the world, having cost the equivalent of one million dollars in 1925.

Some people have said that at times the chandelier will start to swing back and forth and a slight whimper of a man gasping for breath can be heard. Griffith died a lonely and forgotten man who made his home at the Knickerbocker for almost 10 years. Why wouldn't his ghost feel perfectly at home here?

Another actor who called the Knickebocker home was William Frawley, who played Fred Mertz on television's first hit show, *I Love Lucy*. On his way home to the Knickerbocker where he had lived for decades, he had a heart attack on the sidewalk and was carried into the hotel where he died. Some guests have recounted meeting a grumpy man in the lobby to whom they said "hello," but he never replies. Could this have been "grumpy Fred Mertz" from *I Love Lucy*?

Final Thoughts on Hollywood Haunted Hotels

It has been said that if we knew our lives were the entirety of our existence that in all probability we would grasp life with all the gusto we could. Religion promotes a grand and glorious after-life, which means we are supposed to accept the suffering in this one. However, it appears for some, the suffering never ends, as they are trapped in an after-life that is mostly uninspiring. These famous ghosts had an exciting life, but in the end, they are apparently like all ghosts, just spirits in search of a meaning to that which may well have no meaning.

Chapter 4
Texas Terror

Banners bold, glorious, golden

On roofs did float and flow

In a time long, long ago.

Every gentle air that dallied,

In that sweet by-gone day,

Is among the ghosts now so pallid,

As life floated gently away.

Not all ghosts have evil intentions. Some are apparently bent on creating mischief and some just are pleading for compassion. The USA is a nation that prides itself on rugged individualism, which may account for it being less compassionate in so many ways when it comes to elevating its citizens who are mired in poverty at a rate that leads the First World. Some American ghosts apparently long for a little compassion. The St. Anthony Hotel which is located in San Antonio, near the Alamo that stands as a beacon of freedom, apparently harbours some of these weeping ghosts.

For non-North American readers, the Alamo is one of those iconic American patriotic embellishments that are aggrandized as places where freedom was defended, so that all could enjoy the glory of democracy. Unfortunately, it is rarely pointed out that all this freedom that was defended at the Alamo did not include the slaves who were bound to some of its defenders and died there defending what they did not have - freedom. Hypocrisy has always been an undercurrent in the glorification of freedom in the USA unfortunately. The Alamo, itself, is supposed to be filled with ghosts, but near it is the even more ghostly St. Anthony Hotel, which has sometimes been called the "harbourer of the pleading dead."

HAUNTED HOTELS:
TRANSITORY DANCES WITH THE DEAD

The St. Anthony is a five star hotel which apparently also has some 5 star ghosts. Built in 1909, it has been called the grand old lady of San Antonio. The most haunted floor seems to be number 10. Room 1080 appears to harbour the most active ghosts, with some guests reporting that there are faint whimpers heard in the room as if someone is crying. The door, when left ajar seems to always close by itself, and the faucets in the bathroom frequently turn themselves on. Several guests have reported being sound asleep and then feeling the bed sheet slowly pulled off toward the bottom of the bed. They quickly rise and no one is there. Most of the hotel staff refuses to work on this floor as there are cold spots in several rooms and in the hallway. Sometimes, when maids are cleaning, they will turn off their vacuums only to have them mysteriously turn back on. One maid back in the 1940's swears that she was shoved into a closet by unseen hands and cowered there for hours fearing what might be waiting outside. She never went back into room 1080 again. Another maid scrubbed the tub and then saw her name appear on it in ghostly handwriting. She scrubbed the tub again and left the room. When her supervisor inspected the room, she found the employee's name written on the tub. Thinking that the cleaning woman was playing a prank, the supervisor had her scrub that tub all over again while she watched. As they stood there, the name re-appeared. The cleaning lady saw it as a bad omen from a spirit and left to never return.

HAUNTED HOTELS:
TRANSITORY DANCES WITH THE DEAD

The Travis Room is also a place where employees have often reported strange occurrences. When a woman named Morrison owned the hotel back in the 1930's, this room was her office and part-time home. She had a grand piano she played on occasion and her husband loved to sit in a nearby chair and listen. Both the chair and the piano are gone now, but sometimes the staff has reported hearing a piano playing, and also looking over to a chair and seeing the faint outline of a man sitting in it.

The foreboding dark at the top of the stairs leading to the Travis Room offers a challenge even to the most intrepid non-believer in ghosts. One can almost sense something waiting up there to grasp you and shout "boo!"

HAUNTED HOTELS:
TRANSITORY DANCES WITH THE DEAD

In the basement one finds the staff quarters where they change clothes and have a sitting room. Also, this is where the laundry is located in a nearby room. Of course, who likes doing laundry, right? Well, apparently someone finds it so tedious that they can be heard sobbing, but when you enter the room there is no one there. Other times the laundry will be left in the dryer, and when the maid returns, it has been mysteriously removed and placed on top of the machine. Some of the staff refuses to go downstairs to these areas alone.

Texas is a state where packing a gun is as common as changing your underwear on a daily basis. The love of the 2nd Amendment (the right to bear arms) borders on the fanatical among these people who would probably even shoot at a ghost if they were confronted by one. Well, there is a place where they might just get that chance, as the Hotel Galvez on Galveston Island has its share of pesky ghosts flittering all about.

In 1911 the magnificent Hotel Galvez was completed and celebrities and businessmen flocked there. American Presidents

HAUNTED HOTELS:
TRANSITORY DANCES WITH THE DEAD

Franklin D. Roosevelt, Dwight D. Eisenhower and Lyndon B. Johnson stayed there, as did General Douglas MacArthur.

Staff and guests have experienced many unexplained events, leading them to suspect that there are several ghostly residents. The most well known spirit is a lady on the fifth floor. She always asked for room 500. Then, she would go upstairs to the turrets and gaze out at the bay. Her fiancé was at sea, and she was waiting for his return. One day she got word that his ship had sunk and all hands were lost. After a period of denial, she returned to one of the turrets on the top of the hotel and hanged herself. In a sad twist of fate, a month after her death her fiancé returned, as he had survived after all. The staff can sense when she is around as they feel a sudden cold breeze from nowhere. They know she wants no one in room 500, as their equipment malfunctions when trying to make an electronic key for the room. As many times as they try, they cannot make the key. Another sign of the lovelorn lady is a strange light coming from one of the turrets.

Other unexplained activities occur regularly at the hotel. Staff members have been unnerved in the ladies room when the stall door begins to violently rattle, or the commode in the next stall flushes, yet nobody else is in the restroom. Other employees have felt a presence with them on stairways. One extremely strange encounter involved a wall in one of the guest rooms that appeared to bow out into the room several times.

Lynton Viñas

HAUNTED HOTELS:
TRANSITORY DANCES WITH THE DEAD

Austin is a bastion of liberalism in a conservative state, so when it comes to ghosts, people of the left, right, middle-of-the-road or down right anarchists are welcome to experience the specters that dwell at the Driskill Hotel in that city.

Night arrival at the Driskill is recommended for a spine-tinkling thrill of close-encounters of the ghostly kind.

The Driskill, a Romanesque-style building completed in 1886, is the oldest operating hotel in Austin, Texas. The Driskill was conceived and built by Colonel Jesse Driskill, a cattleman who spent his fortune constructing what he loved to call "the finest hotel south of St. Louis."

HAUNTED HOTELS:
TRANSITORY DANCES WITH THE DEAD

The building was built with a special ladies' entrance that allowed female guests to go directly to their rooms; thereby, avoiding the rough and vulgar talk of the cattlemen in the lobby. Unfortunately, there were too few women or men willing to pay the exorbitant prices he charged. At a time when other hotels were 50 cents to one U.S. dollar per night, Driskill charged $2.50 to $5.00, which was extremely steep, even for the rich cattle barons. Following the loss of a great fortune in cattle drives, Driskill was forced to close the hotel in May 1887, after being open only one year. According to legend, he lost the hotel in a poker game in 1888 to his brother-in-law, who became its second owner. Driskill died of a stroke shortly afterward. It has had many owners over the years.

In 1934, future President Lyndon Johnson met his future wife, Claudia "Ladybird" Taylor, for their first date at the Driskill dining room. The Johnsons continued a lifelong love of the Driskill and stayed there often during the rest of their lives. It became his campaign headquarters during his congressional career, especially during his famous 1948 Senate race, and became a favourite place on return trips to Austin during his presidency. He watched the results of the 1964 Presidential Election from its presidential suite and addressed supporters from its ballroom after his victory. Today, the Driskill remains one of the finest hotels in Texas, but the now Hyatt owned facility is considered one of the most haunted hotels in the United States,

Lynton Viñas

featuring a variety of alleged supernatural activities throughout the building, including the spirit of Colonel Driskill himself.

Over the years, the staff and visitors have shared many interesting stories about ghosts, but the funniest involves a paranormal prankster that operates the elevators, moves furniture, pushes guests out of their beds, and hides their belongings. There seems nothing nefarious about this entity's intentions – all it desires is a little frivolity playing pranks on the guests.

The landmark hotel welcomed many celebrity guests who report having brushes with ghosts. Annie Lennox of Eurhythmics fame (method of teaching music) once stayed at The Driskill during a tour. Undecided as to what to wear onstage that night, she laid out two dresses on the bed and took a shower. When she came out of the bathroom, one of the dresses was on the bed and the other had been packed away. Concrete Blonde lead singer Johnette Napolitano also stayed at the hotel. Her song, "Ghost of a Texas Ladies' Man" is supposedly about her encounter with the ghostly Colonel Driskill.

I saw a face in the shower door
A cowboy smile came and faded
I reached for my towel on the floor
I didn't think it was exactly where I'd laid it
"You don't scare me, you don't scare me," I said
To whatever it was floating in the air above my bed
He knew I'd understand

HAUNTED HOTELS:
TRANSITORY DANCES WITH THE DEAD

He was the ghost of a Texas ladies' man

Room 525 is particularly disconcerting as it supposedly was the scene of two suicides that occurred twenty years apart to the exact day, and, in all probability, the exact hour. Known as the "suicide brides", both women committed suicide in the bathroom on their honeymoons by slashing their wrists, for reasons that were never discovered. Was there some sinister force that led to their suicides? People claim to see apparitions in the room of a woman wearing a wedding dress, and to have problems with lights and faucets in the bathroom.

The most popular ghost story deals with four-year-old Samantha Houston, who was the daughter of a U.S. Senator. In 1887, she chased a ball down the grand staircase when she tripped and fell to her death. As a tribute, the hotel owner commissioned a portrait of Samantha that still hangs on the wall of the fifth floor. The painting shows Samantha smiling and holding a bunch of flowers as she clutches a letter. Guests claim to feel dizzy or nauseous when they look at the painting while some report feeling a strange sensation of being lifted off the floor. Others say Samantha tries to communicate through the painting and that if you stare at her long enough, her expression changes. Some people claim to hear her giggling throughout the halls of the hotel, and the sound of her ball bouncing down the stairs. Now, here is the kicker: it turns out that the haunted painting is not a portrait of Samantha Houston. It is a modern replica of a work entitled "Love Letters" by Charles Trevor Garland (1855-1906). Prints of the painting are available everywhere online. Still, there is no accounting of why people get dizzy looking at it, and what of the little girl giggling and bouncing ball?

Still, perhaps the most terrifying tale comes from a maid, who back in the 50's was cleaning a lounge area room. As she diligently worked away, she suddenly smelled the scent of a cigar. The lights became very fuzzy and she slowly turned toward the far wall and there, sitting in a chair was a man puffing on a cigar. She jumped with fright, and the man gave her a sinister smile as she bounded out of the lounge. She returned with one of the desk clerks and the man was gone. That very day, so was she, when she saw a painting of Colonel Driskill on the wall and immediately recognized it as the man in the chair smoking a cigar. This man had appeared there before several times as reported by others and since then he has greeted a few people in that room with his sinister presence, although more often, only the smell of the cigar and the dimming of the lights are present.

It seems that there is a general creepiness about the whole hotel. For example, the walls are lined with incredibly creepy-looking paintings. Is this good marketing or poor marketing? If you think being considered one of the most haunted hotels in the country is good for business - go for it! The biggest problem with these paintings is the intenseness of eyes from the people in them.

HAUNTED HOTELS:
TRANSITORY DANCES WITH THE DEAD

Seriously, would you want to walk down this hallway alone?

No, this is not a publisher's printing mistake. Most people who take a picture of the little girl painting with their cell phones have the image turn sideways no matter how many times they take it in the right position.

Lynton Viñas

HAUNTED HOTELS:
TRANSITORY DANCES WITH THE DEAD

Would you dare stay in the "Suicide Room?"

"Your key to room 525 - have a pleasant sleep."

HAUNTED HOTELS:
TRANSITORY DANCES WITH THE DEAD

Portrait of Colonel Driskill at the top of the stairs.

Lynton Viñas

Chapter 5

Serendipitous Scariness in the South

The boundaries which divide life from death

are at best shadowy and vague. Who shall say where

the one ends and the other begins?... Edgar Allan Poe

The southern USA is often referred to as "The Bible Belt" for good reason. It is an area with churches on every street corner, and a large group of people who genuinely believe that God created the heaven and earth in seven days, that Adam and Eve frolicked in the Garden of Eden with dinosaurs and that evolution is simply an invention of the devil. The older people also cling to a time when there was strict separation of races, and the white man exercised complete control of the society. The myth of mansions and magnolias continues to have a strong grip, almost a stranglehold, on many of these people, as they really believe that the good old days of slavery offered the average white man a more benevolent life where he sat on his veranda sipping mint juleps while "the darkies" toiled in the fields.

The truth is that society never really existed for the majority of white people. The planter class, like today's economic elite, were the 1% of those days who convinced the yeoman farmer (the white poor class) that somehow it was those nasty old "Negroes" who were causing his economic hardship, rather than the moneyed class that hoarded all the wealth. The only difference today is it is the Wall Street market manipulators, bankers and hypocritical politicians who try to convince the Americans that all their problems are caused by the lazy poor, rather than the rich oligarchs.

In the south, many people still wave the confederate flag (the flag of the south in the Civil War) and long for that time when they believe America was great. Bring into this atmosphere of easy manipulation a belief in demons promulgated by old time religion, and you have fertile ground for the intense belief in ghosts. One survey indicated that 52% of people in the south believe in the literal idea that there is a hell in the bowels of the earth where little men with pitch forks and pointed ears go around jabbing people for all eternity. A large percentage of people in the USA, for example, still believe the 9/11 hijackers came from Iraq and that there were weapons of mass destruction there. This is not an indictment of the south, but rather an attempt to open the readers eyes to the mindset of many people who live here, so that some scepticism can be exercised in evaluating the eyewitness accounts of seeing ghosts.

St. James Hotel

Selma, Alabama is in the heart of the old Confederate States of America. It was there that one of the most disgusting examples of how racism was defended by the government was displayed when police brutally beat demonstrators on a bridge that is named after Edmund Winston Pettus, a former Confederate brigadier general, Democratic Party U.S. Senator from Alabama and Grand Dragon of the Alabama Ku Klux Klan. On this bridge an event known as Bloody Sunday occurred on March 7, 1965 when armed policemen attacked civil rights demonstrators with billy clubs and tear gas as they were attempting to march to the Alabama state capital in Montgomery. This incident exposed American hypocrisy to the entire world, as although it preached about democracy, it was steadfastly denying it to over 10% of its own population. Thus, Selma is a town with a history of oppression, and it can be said that it is also a place where ghosts haunt more than just hotels, as there are many ghosts from its inglorious past that hang over the town like a dark cloud of bigotry. Although things have changed somewhat, this city still generates intense feelings in regards to the civil rights movement.

The ghosts here are not black for some mysterious reason, as maybe the idea of segregation still mandates that the races be separated even after death. The St. James Hotel has a long and storied history. Originally called the Hotel Brantly, it has been around since before the Civil War (1861-1865).

The hotel was also once occupied during the Civil War by Union soldiers who burned most of the city, but spared the St. James Hotel. At one time, after the Civil War, a black man named Turner managed the hotel and openly welcomed the notorious outlaw, Jesse James and his gang when they took a break from robbing banks. Apparently, despite having fought in the Civil War for the South and in defence of slavery, the James gang became friends with the freed slave.

It is said that Jesse and his wife, Zee, both haunt the hotel, sometimes even being seen together. James can usually be seen walking alone in and out of certain guest rooms wearing typical cowboy attire of the late 19th century, while Zee's presence is often detected by the strong smell of lavender. Many also hear a dog barking in the courtyard or running through the halls, thought to be the companion of James.

After the James gang departed, the hotel fell on hard times and the doors were closed on the building, and were not reopened for over a century. A group of investors purchased the old hotel and after spending approximately $6 million in restorations, they were able to officially reopen in 1997. This apparently was not well received by the ghosts that had lived in the abandoned building all those years. Almost immediately, people started claiming to have seen the apparition of a man dressed as a cowboy. He is most often seen in the rooms where Jesse James typically stayed - rooms 214, 314, and 315.

Apparently Jesse does get thirsty for alcoholic libations on occasion, as he has been seen in the bar as well. Zee's penchant for lavender has made her presence easy to sense as the smell permeates the area when she is. Although she seems to be a ghost that smells more than appears, there have been instances where a full apparition of her is seen walking the halls. There is a bit of an unfriendly nature about them both, as they can sometimes seem sullen and gruff, never smiling. They appear to be unaware of anyone around them.

There are often sounds of a dog barking and running up and down the hallway, and there are no pets allowed in the hotel. Also, guests often complain about a dog that barks non-stop in the courtyard. When management looks into the complaints, no dog is ever found in the courtyard. Jessie James owned a dog that was his companion for many years. Perhaps, there is a place after death for dogs also. Now, when one of the guests is bitten by this meandering canine, then there will be positive proof that ghosts exist.

One of the most interesting tales comes from a man who stayed at the hotel in 1999. He was in his room when he sensed he was not alone. He walked over to the window and looked out at the the Edmund Pettus Bridge when he felt a hand touch his shoulder and a man's voice uttered, "go ahead and jump." He turned, but there was no one there. Frightened, he sat on the edge of the bed and heard the water running in the bathroom. He walked into the the bathroom where the water was running and no one was there. As he looked down at the tub, a very gruff man's voice said, "Drown yourself." He checked out of the hotel without a word, just flipped the key to room 315 on the desk. 315 was one of the rooms used by Jesse James.

Jesse James awaits your arrival at the St. James!

The Ellis Hotel (Original name: The Winecoff)

This Atlanta, Georgia hotel used to be known as The Winecoff until 1946 when it caught fire and 119 people died in the most deadly hotel fire in history. Located on famous Peachtree Street, the Winecoff was advertised as fireproof. While the hotel's steel structure was fireproof, its interior finishes were combustible, and the exits consisted of a single stairway serving all fifteen floors. A large number of victims jumped to their deaths. One of the victims was William Fleming Winecoff (age 76), the hotel's builder. He lived with his wife for 31 years in suite 1011–1012. He was found dead in a nearby hall.

When The Winecoff was built in 1913, it was the tallest hotel in the country and everyone thought the brick building was invincible, so no fire escapes, alarms or sprinklers were installed. Today, it is considered one of the most haunted hotels in the world. Many guests report seeing mysterious faces and figures in windows and hallways, some even smell smoke or hear loud commotions that sound like people running down the hallways. Workmen and contractors have also noticed that their tools will be moved or missing when no one else is around.

Apparently, the tragedy was so profound that many of those who experienced it and died have lived the experience again and again as ghosts. Some of these experiences date back to the years of renovation after the fire, as workmen reported hearing voices and footsteps in various rooms, as well as the aforementioned mischievous moving of tools.

The staff and guests often report hearing footsteps in the halls when no one is there as well as chilling screams. Some guests have said they were awakened when they smelled smoke but nothing was burning. However, some of the most frightening manifestations are the images of people that appear in the in the windows. The images are distorted and the eyes appear to be pleading as the mouths seem to be screaming in terror. Perhaps it would be a good idea to pull the shades and never look out the windows when staying here.

Eerily, most photos taken of the Ellis, regardless of the quality of the camera, come out blurry.

Crescent Hotel – Eureka Springs, Arkansas

The Crescent Hotel was built in 1886 as a resort for the rich and famous, but quickly fell into disrepair and was abandoned. In 1908, it was reopened as the Crescent College and Conservatory for Young Women. This institution closed down in 1924, and then opened again in 1930 as a junior college. After the college closed in 1934, the Crescent was leased as a summer hotel. In 1937, a new owner, Norman G. Baker, turned it into a hospital and health resort. Baker, a millionaire inventor and radio personality, styled himself as a doctor, despite having no medical training. He claimed to have discovered a number of cures for various ailments, including cancer, and launched frequent attacks on organized medicine, which he accused of being corrupt and profit-driven. Having been run out of Iowa for practicing medicine without a license, Baker moved his cancer patients to Arkansas and advertised his new health resort at the Crescent. His cure consisted primarily of drinking the area's natural spring water. In 1940, federal charges were filed against Baker for mail fraud and he spent four years in prison. The Crescent Hotel was left ownerless until 1946. In the spring of that year, it was purchased by four men who turned it into a hotel.

A variety of stories have been told about what actually occurred at the "hospital" during the time that Baker was running his practice; however, none of these have ever been officially documented. These stories include claims that many human experiments were performed at the resort and that during later years, when the hotel was being renovated, human skeletons were found as well as jars that contained body parts which were preserved. There are tales of experiments that Baker performed on patients with brain tumors in which he exposed the brain by opening the skull and pouring his "miracle cure" directly on the brain. The bodies were assumed to be hidden until they could be disposed of by incineration during the night. The hotel remained closed until the year of 1946 when it was taken over by new owners and renovations began which have continued over the years and today, the hotel has earned the reputation of being one of the best places to stay when visiting Eureka Springs.

Numerous employees and guests have experienced strange occurrences over the years. Room 218 seems to be one of the most active. Some employees and guests have reported seeing strange shadows in the room. A few people who slept in 218 claimed to have been physically shaken on the shoulder while in bed, but when they opened their eyes, no one as there. Other reports include slamming doors, strange sounds and odd physical sensations.

Some guests claim to have seen a rather tall heavy-set stern-looking nurse who is thought to have worked for Baker. Other guests have reported hearing the sound of a gurney being pushed down the hallway. An old antique telephone switchboard that was on display in the lobby was removed after complaints from the staff that it kept buzzing, even though it was not used. One person instinctively picked up the earpiece only to be told to come to a locked room in the basement. The manager got a key and when they went down to the room there was a phone on a desk that was off the hook. No one had been in the room for many years.

HAUNTED HOTELS:
TRANSITORY DANCES WITH THE DEAD

Guest and employees claim to have talked to a woman in room 419 who says she is a cancer patient. She gets up from her chair and walks into the bathroom. When the bathroom is checked, no one is there. Other guests report seeing in the Crystal Dining Room individuals dressed in Victorian era clothing either seated at the tables or appearing in the mirrors. The images appear only late at night and when the hotel is deathly quiet. The images are only there for an instant.

Finally, the "doctor" himself has appeared on occasion, apparently returning to the place where he plied his nefarious trade. One guest said the doctor asked him if he wanted a colonic wash to remove cancer cells. The guest wisely refused.

This hotel is in America, right? So, with the entrepreneurial spirit of capitalism, the hotel now offers ghost tours seven nights a week.

How about a quiet evening by the fireplace,

with a ghost, of course

HAUNTED HOTELS:
TRANSITORY DANCES WITH THE DEAD

The ghosts at the Crescent know no season, but it is rumoured

that more apparitions occur in winter.

The Myrtles Plantation Bed and Breakfast Hotel

HAUNTED HOTELS:
TRANSITORY DANCES WITH THE DEAD

The unique amalgam of ethnicities and cultures has created an eclectic storehouse of music, language and food in Louisiana. The French language is so abundantly used that Louisiana officially recognizes both English and French. Away from the vibrant, almost insane exuberance of Bourbon Street in New Orleans, one can find small hamlets here that are the embodiment of that aforementioned myth of mansions and magnolias. Sitting on the porches of antebellum mansions and sipping mint juleps is a past-time for many tourists who have discovered the quite, quaint serenity of places seemingly lost in time. Here, one can experience a past that is over-romanticized and far too often embellished. Oh, and maybe one can also converse with a ghost!

The Myrtles Plantation Hotel is a historic home and former antebellum plantation in St. Francisville, Lousiana that was built in 1796. Located on a small hill, it is built in the Creole cottage style that characterizes many Louisiana plantation houses. The entry doors are surrounded with a transom and sidelights, showcasing original hand-painted stained glass, etched and patterned after the cross to allegedly ward off evil. The main feature of the Myrtles is the 125-foot long veranda that extends the entire length of the facade and wraps around the southern end of the house. It has 22 rooms spread over two floors.

The Myrtles Plantation was built by General David Bradford on 600 acres and was named Laurel Grove. Bradford lived there alone for several years, until President John Adams pardoned him for his role in a rebellion in Pennsylvania. He then moved his wife Elizabeth and their five children to the plantation from Pennsylvania. Upon Bradford's death in 1808, his widow Elizabeth continued running the plantation until 1817, when she handed the management to Clarke Woodruff, one of Bradford's former law students, who had married her daughter, Sara.

When Elizabeth Bradford died in 1831, Clarke Woodruff and his surviving daughter, Mary Octavia, moved to Covington, Louisiana, and left a caretaker to manage the plantation. In 1834, Woodruff sold the plantation, the land and its slaves. The new owners changed the name to "The Myrtles" after the crepe myrtles that majestically grew in the vicinity. The Myrtles survived the brutal American Civil War, but the plantation was heavily in debt; therefore, it was sold in 1886 and passed through a number of owners afterwards, none of them very successful in its operation

In the early part of the 20th-century, the land surrounding the house was divided among heirs. In the 1950s, the house only was sold to Marjorie Munson, who apparently noticed odd things happening, and she became almost paranoid if forced to stay alone there. The plantation went through several more ownership changes. Author Frances Kermeen wrote a book about the Myrtles Plantation, naming it as the most haunted house in America. Regardless, today's current owners continue to operate it as a B&B hotel and popular tourist attraction due to its association with paranormal activity. It has been featured in many books, magazines, newspapers and television shows.

The plantation house is rumoured to be on top of an old Native American burial ground. To date, there have been 12 resident ghosts identified. Supposedly, at least 10 murders have also been committed here, the most notable one being William Drew Winter. He was an attorney who lived at the plantation from 1865 until 1871. He was shot by a stranger. After being shot, he staggered inside the house and died trying to climb the stairs. He died on the 17th step of the stairs, and that is the exact spot where some guests and employees claim to hear the sound of someone seeming to be crawling up the stairs. Handprints are also sometimes seen on the carpet at the 17th step.

In 2002, the television show, *Unsolved Mysteries,* filmed an episode about the alleged haunting of the plantation. According to host, the late Robert Stack, the production crew experienced technical difficulties during the production of the segment.

Mirrors have long had a reputation for connecting the world of the living to the world of the dead. There is a 200 year old mirror at the Myrtles that has seemingly been a grand conduit for entities trying to communicate from the beyond. There are many stories about the mirror, but the most common one deals with a slave who poisoned the Woodruff family that owned the plantation. Sara Woodruff, the owner, and her two daughters died and were cursed by the slave to forever be trapped in the mirror.

HAUNTED HOTELS:
TRANSITORY DANCES WITH THE DEAD

Mysterious finger prints appear on the mirror and strange drip marks run the length of it, and no amount of cleaning can eliminate the marks permanently as they keep coming back.

The slave is also rumoured to have been seen about the grounds at various times, as she was hanged on the property for the murder of the Woodruffs. She materializes as a haggard, morose woman who seems to be looking for something. Perhaps she is looking for a mirror to tidy herself up!

HAUNTED HOTELS:
TRANSITORY DANCES WITH THE DEAD

Many years ago, before digital cameras, a teacher and her students posed for photos in front of the hotel. Later, when the teacher went over her photos, she noticed a chilling guest in one. A little girl, dressed in her Ante-bellum clothing, was peering out the window behind them. The odd thing is that this was not the first nor last time this happened. Research into the little girl's identity has been extensive and it is assumed she is the ghost of a young girl who died there of yellow fever in 1868, despite the efforts of a Voodoo practitioner to save her. She rarely appears anywhere, except at the window, but has been seen upstairs on occasion.

Other unusual occurrences reported by guests and employees include broken clocks that tick, beds that shake and levitate, footsteps, portraits whose expressions change and a crystal chandelier that sways and jingles even when every window is shut and there is no breeze.

Summary

Fact or fiction is often hard to decipher as that which was once fiction, over the years, morphs into fact. In a world where Donald Trump's legendary counsellor, Kelly Ann Conway, once coined the phrase "alternative fact" rather than espouse the true word which is "lie," it is understandable why fiction can become fact and fact can become fiction. Author, Wayne Frye, who was born in North Carolina and lived there until he was 18, has said, "In the south, the past is never dead. It is not even the past. In a place where the miseries of slavery, tenant farming and being bound to the barons of greed in textile mills kept the majority in abject poverty, somehow, those times have been romanticized as grand and glorious."

The ghosts of the past hold a fascination for the living, particularly in the South, where superstition and the supernatural are more readily embraced. This book is not promoting belief or disbelief – just presenting the facts as they are known. As William Faulkner said of ghosts, "Shadows of the deceased abound in Southern culture; because there the light of life is so dim for so many that the after-life is often preferable to real life."

Chapter 6

The Ghosts of What Could Have Been

Wanderers in that happy valley,

Through luminous windows, saw

Spirits moving musically

To a lute's well-tuned law,

Round about a throne where, sitting,

Goblins laughed at what might befall.

To the walking dead it was befitting,

To joyfully do the devil's bidding.

There is a false notion that the original immigrants came to America in search of religious freedom. The actual truth is they came to practice their own brand of harsh religion free of any restraints. They wanted forced adherence to their dogmatic beliefs. To this end, the religious leaders refined the art of coercion.

HAUNTED HOTELS:
TRANSITORY DANCES WITH THE DEAD

New England is the place where so-called witches were burned at the stake, where transgressors were locked in stocks, where those who defied authority were shunned and where people were placed on the rack to illicit confessions – all in the name of God. Is it any wonder that the society that existed back in the early days of America embraced the ideas of demons prancing about looking for souls to steal? And today, those demons still apparently inhabit a few places in New England, some of which are hotels.

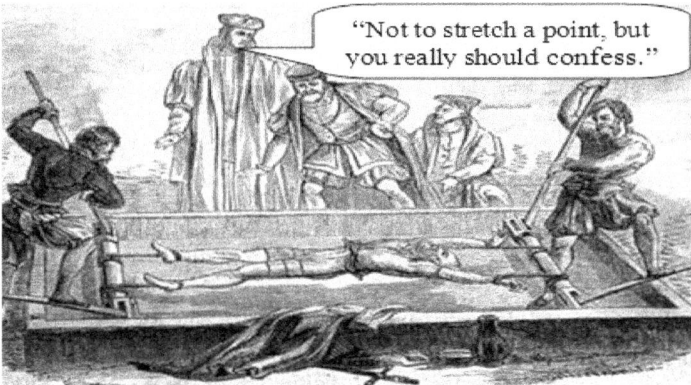

HAUNTED HOTELS:
TRANSITORY DANCES WITH THE DEAD

Oddly, today, the New England states are among the most liberal places in the USA. However, it is also a place where the spirits of the dead roam about in the forests, the churches, the homes, the public buildings, the ancient grave yards, and, of course, hotels.

Beal House Inn

Littleton, New Hampshire is a quaint little village where a farmhouse was built in 1833 at the end of town, but an enterprising descendent of Mrs. Beal, the original owner, turned it into an inn in 1933. Over the years the inn has seen many owners, but in 2001, the new owners began extensive renovations and one of the owner's mothers came over from Europe to spend a couple nights. She settled down for what she hoped would be a peaceful sleep. Unfortunately, it wasn't, and as she sat at the kitchen table the next morning she informed them that there was something strange about the room. Unafraid, she spent the rest of her nights in the room, and refused to reveal what was happening, only saying that there was some strange activity in the room.

An energetic housekeeper was painting when she felt some pressure on her hip, thinking it was one of the owners as they were in and out throughout the day, she was going to move to the side, but something held (or forced) her there for a few seconds. She turned and there was no one there, but when she finally caught her breath and resumed painting, the same pressure happened on the other side. She finally put down her brush and stopped, waiting for the owners to return. When they did, she handed them the paint brush and said, "good luck" and left.

Strange, unintelligible male voices have been heard in the common room where people have been congregating. The owners have reported seeing a shadow about the house, and when it appears the room gets really warm. Apparently, it is a common for visitors to be awakened by the loud sounds of slamming doors or hearing heavy footsteps stomping up and down stairs late at night. Each time that someone launches an immediate investigation, nobody is there. At least no living person is there making the noise. Maybe Mrs. Beal has never left.

Have a seat in the Garden Room, and maybe Mrs. Beal will sit with you for a lively discussion on what it is like "on the other side."

HAUNTED HOTELS:
TRANSITORY DANCES WITH THE DEAD

<u>Lizzie Borden Bed</u>
<u>and Breakfast</u>

Lizzie Borden – Circa 1890

Lizzie Borden had an axe

She gave her mother 40 whacks

When she saw what she had done

She gave her father 41

Lizzie Andrew Borden (1860 – 1927) was an American woman who gained infamy in being tried and acquitted for the 1892 axe murders of her father and stepmother in Fall River, Massachusetts. The case was a world-wide sensation. Following her release from the prison in which she had been held during the trial; Borden remained a resident of Fall River, Massachusetts for the rest of her life, despite facing significant ostracism. The Commonwealth of Massachusetts elected to charge no one else with the murder of Andrew and Abby Borden and speculation about the crimes still continues.

Lizzie's father was an immensely wealthy man who owned textile mills and was president of two banks. Despite his wealth he was known for frugality and also for cruelty toward his family.

HAUNTED HOTELS:
TRANSITORY DANCES WITH THE DEAD

Three years after the death of Lizzie's mother, her father married again. Lizzie stated, during police questioning, that she believed that her stepmother was after her father's money. In May 1892 Lizzie's father, believing that pigeons in the barn were attracting local children to hunt them, killed the pigeons with a hatchet. Lizzie had recently built a roost for the pigeons and was upset at their deaths. A family argument prompted Lizzie to take an extended vacation in nearby New Bedford. Returning to Fall River the week before the murders, Lizzie chose to stay in a rooming house for four days before returning to the family residence. Lizzie's father was giving away a lot of property to his new wife at this time, and this infuriated Lizzie and her sister. Within a few days, the same axe that Lizzie's father used to kill the pigeons was used to kill Lizzie's stepmother and father. The murders were particularly brutal with multiple blows delivered to each person, making them almost unrecognizable. Though no bloody clothing was found, a few days after the murder Lizzie burned a dress, saying that it had been ruined when she brushed against fresh paint. Lizzie's defence attorney was one of the greatest lawyers of the time, and, with a remarkable presentation, he spellbound the courtroom and jurors with such an effect that within one-half hour they returned a not-guilty verdict. Still, the majority of people all across America assumed that Lizzie was indeed guilty. It was categorized as the trial of the century, and Lizzie never denied or admitted guilt.

HAUNTED HOTELS:
TRANSITORY DANCES WITH THE DEAD

With that bit of background, we can now move on to the house where these murders occurred, which is a bed and breakfast hotel and museum. Lizzie Borden Bed and Breakfast was voted one of the scariest places on earth. Even those who are sceptics, when in the house say "something strange is going on here," and tales of phantom footsteps and unnatural gusts of wind, especially when guests use the Ouija Board in the sitting room, abound.

Of course, most visitors here anticipate an encounter with Lizzie's pulp-headed parents, but none have been reported. Lizzie's stepmother's death room is the most popular rental in the house. The owner says that there are a few people make it through the night in the room but many people slip out around 2:00 AM. Unfortunately for those who run for the exit there is no breakfast, which is a shame, since it is exactly the same breakfast the Borden's ate on the morning of their murders.

HAUNTED HOTELS:
TRANSITORY DANCES WITH THE DEAD

Perhaps the scariest tale comes from the owner, who in 2004 was actually scared out of the house for a night. She had nodded off to sleep on the sofa in the parlour room where Lizzie's father was killed and awoke at 3 A.M. She peeked down into the front entryway and took in the shadows cast by a special old chandelier that was always lit. She glanced to the right of the chandelier and noticed another shadow in the hallway. As she stared in disbelief, the shadow of a woman in turn-of-the-century dress slowly ascended the stairs. She got up from the sofa, walked to the front door and left, not returning until the next morning. No doubt, the ghost felt sorry for scaring her and prepared wonderful breakfast which was waiting.

Orleans Waterfront Inn

Not nearly as infamous as the Lizzie Borden Hotel, but one that may actually have even more strange tales is the Orleans Waterfront Inn in Orleans, Massachusetts. It was actually a brothel back in the 1920's, so the good times really rolled here. The inn reportedly experiences all the slamming doors, gusts of inexplicable cold air and footsteps that other haunted inns boast, but there is also photographic evidence. At a high School 25th reunion party in the inn several years ago, the owner snapped a group photo. When the revellers saw it later, they were bewildered and astonished by a beautiful woman in the photo who was not a class member. She was to the right and in 1920's period dress.

HAUNTED HOTELS:
TRANSITORY DANCES WITH THE DEAD

Apparently, this is the ghost of a girl named Hannah who happily occupies the house. The owner's first acquaintance with Hannah was rather interesting. He often sleeps on the sofa in case a guest needs something at night. Once he awoke when a naked woman came down the stairs. He and the woman exchanged hellos, and he fell back asleep, assuming it was a free-spirited guest that the clerk had checked in during his absence. He did not think of the encounter again until he received a phone call from a passing motorist several days later, who warned him to put curtains into the fourth-floor window. When asked why, the man answered that he could see a naked woman dancing around in the room. This was particularly interesting, as there were no guests in the fourth floor room. Now, I am sure the male readers will be flocking to the Orleans Waterfront Inn. Good luck on finding this naked ghost!

HAUNTED HOTELS:
TRANSITORY DANCES WITH THE DEAD

<u>Yankee Pedlar Inn</u>

In 1890, Frank Conley opened the Conley Hotel in Torrington, Connecticut. His wife was the manager while Frank was a jack of all trades who kept things up and running. Throughout much of the first half of the 20th century, it was managed as a family business. After the couple died, the hotel was taken over by their niece. It was later expanded and renovated after it was sold by the Conley family. It became the Yankee Pedlar Inn in 1956 when the hotel was combined with the restaurant next door.

One of inn's the most haunted rooms is number 353, where Alice Conley died. Some people experience a loud voice telling them to get out, and others report cold spots in the room. In other rooms there are tales of random disembodied voices, a chair that rocks on its own in the lobby late at night and doors that close without assistance from human hands. Many guests report televisions turning on at all hours of the night.

HAUNTED HOTELS:
TRANSITORY DANCES WITH THE DEAD

The Yankee Pedlar has scary hallways
like so many of the other hotels.

Hawthorne Hotel

The dark history of the 1692 Salem Witch Trials has given Salem, Massachusetts a reputation for intolerance and religious fanaticism. Its dark history is a thing of the past, as, like the rest of Massachusetts today, it is a bastion of progressive thinking. However, for a brief time, it was the very essence of bigoted intolerance and an example of how hysteria can sweep up good citizens in frenzied paranoia as has been so prevalent in the USA, especially since 9/11/2001. Twenty people were accused of witchcraft and sentenced to death by Judge John Hawthorne. One of his descendants, famous writer Nathaniel Hawthorne, was the inspiration for the Hawthorne Hotel. Ironically, Nathaniel Hawthorne was a master at ghost storytelling.

HAUNTED HOTELS:
TRANSITORY DANCES WITH THE DEAD

When the need for a modern hotel became evident, the town of Salem sold more than half a million dollars worth of stock for a proposed hotel. Built entirely from the funds earned by selling stock, it was decided to name the hotel after Massachusetts most famous writer. The Hawthorne opened on July 23, 1925 with Nathaniel Hawthorne's granddaughter in attendance. Since then, there have been many strange occurrences here.

In a room referred to as the library, tables are set up for weddings and other events. One staff member, having set up the room for an event, returned to the location only to discover the room had been rearranged with tables and chairs stacked and moved about. The employee refused to work night shifts after this experience, and others have encountered the exact same phenomena over the years.

Room 325 and Suite 612 have had some strange reports of their bathroom door suddenly closing, and then hearing the sound of running water. Opening the door, the guests discover the water running but no one there.

Other guests report of turning the lights off only to have them immediately switched back on as they walk away. There have been complaints of objects, such as keys or cell phones that have been put one place before going to bed being mysteriously found in another place in the morning. Sometimes, in the middle of the night, guests have felt the bed sheet being pulled off them toward the foot of the bed.

HAUNTED HOTELS:
TRANSITORY DANCES WITH THE DEAD

Some guests claim to have had someone sit on the end of their bed or they awoke because they thought they were being touched. The hallways often have dark shadows about and sometimes apparitions are seen.

The whole sixth floor is reputedly haunted with some investigators intonating captains from the Salem Marine Society, which once met there, are causing mischief in the afterlife. There is a rumour that these sailors also toy with the nautical themed ships wheel in the restaurant. Several people have claimed to have seen the ship's wheel turn with no one being near it. Some of those who have seen it have stopped the wheel only to see it continue turning after they walk away.

Ghosts, real or imagined, haunt us all in one way or another. There are the ghosts of lost opportunities, the ghosts of lost loves, the ghosts of regrets, and there are the ghosts of what could have been.

HAUNTED HOTELS:
TRANSITORY DANCES WITH THE DEAD

Chapter 7

The Rumba of Rambling Latin Ghosts

Travellers, now, within the valley,

Through the red-litten windows see

Vast forms that move fantastically

To a discordant melody;

While, like a ghastly rapid river,

Through the pale door

A hideous throng rush out forever,

And laugh - but smile no more.

It is said that there is a certain programmed pattern, a genuine well-coordinated rhythm to everything; and that we are all waltzing with ghosts of the past, present and future in the ballroom of life. There is a very special rhythm that is unique to South America, and the same can be said of its ghosts who dance to a tune all their own.

HAUNTED HOTELS:
TRANSITORY DANCES WITH THE DEAD

<u>Eden Hotel</u>

While the USA was concentrating on getting the Nazi scientists out of Germany to help with their space programme, some of the more nefarious German war criminals made their way to Argentina. One hotel there was notorious for welcoming these fugitives from justice who were trying to avoid prosecution for war crimes.

In 1937, the following silver anniversary congratulatory telegram was sent to the Eden Hotel owners: *"Mr. and Mrs. Eichhorn, To my comrades in battle during difficult times for your Silver Anniversary. Warm Wishes, Adolf Hitler."*

In the early 20th century, the Eden Hotel in Cordoba La Falda, Argentina was frequented by the rich and famous. It was visited by Albert Einstein, the Prince of Wales and many Argentine presidents. Roberto Balkhc, a German hotelier, built this hotel on vast land with great scenery. It opened in 1899 as a place for the wealthy and privileged, but when the Eichorn family, which was an ardent supporter of Hitler, took over the hotel in the 1920's it became a Nazi haven. During World War II, Walter and Ida Eichorn, along with their supporters, held secret meetings and fitted the hotel's roof with radio antenna so they could hear Hitler's live speeches transmitted from Germany.

Under pressure from the USA, when Argentina declared war on Germany in 1945, the government closed the hotel and confiscated the property. In the years that it was abandoned, it

Lynton Viñas

exuded the aura of being haunted. Ghost sightings in the hotel include the apparitions of a little girl, presumably Eichorn's daughter, babies, servers and others who died inside. The ghosts whisper, slam the doors and let out random noises.

Today, the hotel is closed and there are tours conducted by the municipality. There have been, for years since the end of World War II, reports of strange ghost like apparitions floating about in various parts of the old hotel, and sometimes visitors have reported being tapped on the shoulder, only to turn around and see no one there.

The Eden still stands majestic among the nearby mountains, but at night sinister things seem to be afoot.

Hotel del Salto – Tequendama Falls, Columbia

Near a scenic waterfall in the jungles of Colombia sits a strange sight: A massive stone European-style mansion built right into the side of a hill, overlooking the Bogota River and the Tequendama Falls. Once one of the premier destinations in the entire country, it has sat abandoned for decades.

HAUNTED HOTELS:
TRANSITORY DANCES WITH THE DEAD

As nature reclaimed the structure, inside and out, rumours of something sinister swirled in the countryside. The building was designed and constructed as a mansion in 1923 for some of Colombia's wealthiest citizens. It was known for its great beauty and magnificent view of the falls.

The pounding sound of the waterfall which is approximately 140 metres high (over 450 feet) can sometimes be almost deafening, but apparently the ghosts which are supposed to reside in the old abandoned mansion hotel are not bothered by it.

Lynton Viñas

HAUNTED HOTELS:
TRANSITORY DANCES WITH THE DEAD

Every bit as sinister looking as the Bates Mansion in the Alfred Hitchcock movie, Psycho, this foreboding place is said to be home to spirits that refuse to go quietly into eternal sleep.

After thirty years of decadent indulgence by the wealthy people who owned it, the place became a financial burden and the site of people actually committing suicide by walking above the falls and jumping into the swirling pools below made them decide to convert it into a hotel. However, the construction, which started in 1950, was very slow, and the increasingly polluted Bogota River gave off a horrendous smell. Also, workers complained of strange noises and having their tools constantly moved.

So scared were the workers that, when they were asked to work nights, they refused, saying that there were too many strange noises and that doors would open and close on their own. Work slowed to a crawl, and when it was finished, the rumours of ghosts seemed to financially doom the hotel. It was finally closed in 1970 and nature, as it is prone to do, reclaimed this monument to excess, and now it is a tourist attraction, but no tourists seem interested in visiting at night.

There is a legend that those who jump into the whirlpool are forever trapped within the confines of the valley, and many of the ghosts have apparently elected to take up residence in the hotel. After all, accommodations are extremely cheap!

La Posada del Sol

It appears that just because a hotel closes, it does not mean all the guests leave. In the heart of Mexico City stands another abandoned hotel called La Posada del Sol. This is a place that like the neighbourhood around it has been in decline for many years. The poor residents in the area look upon it with awe as a place where ghosts linger in perpetuity searching for a way out of their purgatory, seemingly forever trapped in this tomb-like edifice that is sombre and cold like the stone from which it was built. Still, there are those who revere it, making a shrine to one little girl ghost there, and actually leaving candy for her to enjoy as she flitters about this lonely place in the midst of one of Mexico City's most populated ghettos.

HAUNTED HOTELS:
TRANSITORY DANCES WITH THE DEAD

A place worthy of the many rumours of apparitions, it is seemingly lost in the nether world of ghosts and goblins. It has never been put to its original use, nor inhabited for a lengthy period of time, out of fear. Of course, whether these fears are well-founded or not are subject to debate. Mexico is a Catholic nation, where people, the poor in particular, with nothing else to rely on but religion, cling steadfastly to ideas of demons that not only inhabit places like La Posada del Sol but are capable of capturing people's souls. These people, like so many of its northern neighbour's people, cling to the hope of an after-life, any life that would be better then the burden laden life of constantly struggling just for the mere essentials that are like luxuries to the people caught in the iron-like grip of poverty.

Each stride through the grounds is made with quiet trepidation, as visitors seem leery of awakening the spirits haunting the hotel.

HAUNTED HOTELS:
TRANSITORY DANCES WITH THE DEAD

La Posada del Sol is a monumental mid-20th century building that blends colonial architecture with Art Nouveau, making for an interesting, if somewhat bizarre mismatch of styles that make the visitor seem lost, not in the grandeur of the place, but in the starkness that makes it seem like a tomb rather than a hotel.

La Posada del Sol is a fascinatingly pretentious project from a man with grandiose ideas named Fernando Saldaña Galván that was never put to its original use. Saldaña Galván intended it to be a refuge for artists and intellectuals; however, cost overruns led him to think a way to complete the project and satisfy creditors was to convert it into a grand hotel. The only trouble was that it appeared more like a monastery than a hotel.

The Posada del Sol on Niños Heroes in Colonia Doctores started out keeping pace with Saldaña's vision, but he seemed to forget you only got building permits by bribing the inspectors. At times, the excessive bribe requests were exceeding his funds; consequently, his finances deteriorated. Destiny was not his ally, as debts mounted and delays went on for years, only acerbating the problem. His life's work, to quote author Anthony Wright, "was a ship forever on the horizon, never out of sight, never landing until it was finally mocked to death by time."

Saldaña committed suicide by hanging himself in front of a statue of Saint Francis of Assisi that is on the grounds of La Posada del Sol. Before doing so, however, he had an inscription carved into a stone within the premises, a part of which reads:

HAUNTED HOTELS:
TRANSITORY DANCES WITH THE DEAD

"I recommend that the vain and the angry without merit be appraised, who tried to humiliate me and overloaded me with difficulties, or climbed over me to increase their own ostentation and patrimony, while I have worked with no truce and no hope. F.S.G. - February 22, 1945."

Saldaña's body was found swinging from a tree across from this statue of Sr. Francis of Assisi.

In the years following Saldaña's death, the building became home to a variety of organizations that eventually vacated the premises with complaints of strange noises, unusual occurrences and a few apparitions, among them Saldaña, who would apparently appear in hallways, and sometimes even be heard to whisper softly, "They ruined me" to people in the library. Mannequins have been placed all throughout in homage to the ghosts that are supposed to haunt the place. One of the most haunted rooms is what is referred to as the little girl's room, a place where a child supposedly died when she got lost. Her photo graces a mini altar where people leave candy, as it is said that her ghost has been seen wondering about the grounds, occasionally asking visitors for some candy.

The affectionately named "Little Girl Altar," where people leave candy for the child who supposedly died in the room by herself, hopelessly lost and starving.

HAUNTED HOTELS:
TRANSITORY DANCES WITH THE DEAD

There is a feeling here that sends shivers up and down your spine. A stroll through the grounds is a journey into the macabre. Each stone faced statue is so lifeless, so cold, so filled with anger that to look upon any of them is frightening, causing one to almost see the statues pulsating back and forth as if trying to bore evil into the mind of the viewer. The heart races and there is a critical urge to leave, but the pull of the place seems to trap you, make you feel that you cannot leave, that you must wander about more, embracing the pull of those who refuse to pass over to the other side.

Even the art on the walls was conceived by Saldaña, and it seems his ghost is a part of each mural that reaches out with evil intentions to wrap your mind, body and soul in the embrace of the macabre.

Notice the sternness of the white man who has conquered the Aztecs and has brought ruin just as corrupt bureaucrats brought ruin to Saldaña.

HAUNTED HOTELS:
TRANSITORY DANCES WITH THE DEAD

The lifespan of operations as a hotel was a mere eight months, but it has had a lasting legacy that simply has gripped the entire city with its reputation for ghostly manifestations that permeate the grounds. There is a theory that the entire structure is based on the number 33, and that the Free Mason Society saw it as a glorification of their organization. Those who agree with this tend to emphasize the symbols that are hidden inside of the building. Repetitions of the number 33, pentagrams, pregnant virgins and a cryptic alphabet all reinforce the idea that there is something unholy about the place.

There is also a church on the grounds, but it seems to be a desecration of what is holy. There is a pentagram over the basilica and on the floor that extends over the surface. Even the cross seems to be diminished before evil.

Lynton Viñas

HAUNTED HOTELS:
TRANSITORY DANCES WITH THE DEAD

Twelve statues of owls with eyes made of precious gems watch from the heights above the pentagram. The space above is decorated with zodiac signs sculpted in the stone and there is a door on the second floor that leads directly to the main chambers of the hotel where Saldaña lived and contemplated day in and day out the fate of his beloved edifice that was sinking into ruin as a magnificent work of architecture while his own personal ruin was ever imminent. Was the antipathy toward his project partly because he was perceived as unholy in a nation where the church held and, in many ways, still holds great sway over the government? Was it in truth the lack of bribes he was willing to pay, or was it pressure from the church that saw the place as an abomination, a plight on the glory of God?

Was Saldaña, as rumours made out, some type of secret devil worshipper? And is it true, as has been rumoured and apparently hushed up, that over forty human skulls and bones were found in a secret chamber, perhaps the remains of those who were sacrificed to the devil? It has also been rumoured that notoriously corrupt police chief, Negro Durazo, in his reign of terror between 1976 and 1982 may have used the place as a torture chamber for student protestors who disappeared without a trace, which leads many ghosts theorists to intonate that the souls of the poor tortured students are roaming the grounds, trapped forever within the confines of this edifice that stands as a solemn and perverse monument to evil.

HAUNTED HOTELS:
TRANSITORY DANCES WITH THE DEAD

Regardless of which theory one embraces, this place has a very dark, sordid and mysterious history that leads even the security personnel who guard the place to never venture inside once the sun goes down, as they fear the rumba of rambling Latin ghosts.

Chapter 8

Rollicking, Frolicking Canadian Ghosts

Time held me green and dying,

Though I sang in my chains like the sea.

(Dylan Thomas, 1952)

Located in the heart of Banff National Park, a UNESCO World Heritage Site, rising majestically like an ancient phoenix on the plains of time is the world famous Fairmont Banff Springs Hotel standing as a hallmark of granduer in the picturesque alpine town of Banff, Alberta. Called Canada's Castle in the Rockies, it is one of the most breathtaking hotels in the world, and of course, after all these years, it has naturally seen some visits from the other world. Although not considered malevolent, the ghosts here can still send chills up and down the spine. Of course, ghosts can be either/or malevolent and playful. One might ask the question: "Why would any ghost ever want to leave such a grand, glorious and beautiful place?"

HAUNTED HOTELS:
TRANSITORY DANCES WITH THE DEAD

Lynton Viñas

HAUNTED HOTELS:
TRANSITORY DANCES WITH THE DEAD

"Canada is a grand and glorious country, where diversity is not decried, ridiculed or demeaned. Canada is the microcosm of humanity in all its glory, where the church and state are separated irresolutely in defence of a person's right to reach their full potential unrestrained by convention. This is freedom in all its grandeur!" ....J. Wayne Frye, Author

Canada is consistently rated as one of the top three countries in the world in which to live. It embraces, as the above quote from Wayne Frye indicates, the great diversity of humanity and offers a non-judgemental attitude that is welcoming and open, so is it any wonder that even its ghosts seem more equalitarian than those in other places.

The Banff Springs Hotel, like so many other Canadian hotels, was built by a railroad. It was the vision of Canadian Pacific Railways' CEO, William Van Horne, who started construction on this magnificent structure in the spring of 1888. Since its opening, it has attracted the rich and famous from all over the world, and, of course, some of us ordinary folks, too. Some of the famous guests, including Marilyn Monroe and Helen Keller, must have liked the place so much they have visited regularly after their deaths. However, the hotel, apparently assuming ghosts are not good for business, absolutely denies that there are any ghosts about. Frankly, I believe a good marketer could promote the fact that you might get a glimpse of Marilyn Monroe as an inducement to attract customers.

HAUNTED HOTELS:
TRANSITORY DANCES WITH THE DEAD

This hotel has what has been described by some as *the missing room*. In room 873 on the eighth floor, according to hotel lore, a man checked in with his wife and daughter. He promptly killed his wife and daughter and then committed suicide. The spirits of the mother and daughter are supposed to haunt the room. There were reports of violent shrieks in the night, and maids reported finding bloody fingerprints on numerous occasions. In response to these claims, the room was sealed off and a wall replaced the door. Still, you will get firm denials from hotel management, but no explanation as to why all the other floors have rooms with the number 73 in them but not on the eight floor. Despite sealing off the room, some guests complain of weird sounds emanating from behind the wall.

Some of the hallways have small alcoves. One in particular is referred to as the spooky painting alcove, where some guests claim to have seen what appeared to be a transparent-like gown just floating behind the lamp. Others claim that the woman's right eye in the panting seems to be following you.

HAUNTED HOTELS:
TRANSITORY DANCES WITH THE DEAD

Another ghostly presence is supposed to walk the halls late at night, but never with any ill intent. It is assumed to be the ghost of Sam McCauley, a bellman from Scotland who, when he knew he was dying, vowed to return from the beyond to forever walk the halls of the Banff Springs Hotel. Mysterious dimming and brightening hallway lamps, elevator doors opening and closing when there is no one pushing the button, and people sensing a presence in the hallway have been reported. A few hotel guests have even mentioned that they were helped by a bellman with a deep Scottish accent in what appeared to be a very old uniform.

Spectres include a bartender who encourages people to drink no more, as they appear drunk, and even a headless man who, despite having no eyes is apparently looking for his head, and with a bagpipe around his shoulder he also occasionally plays, rousing people from their sleep.

So famous is one ghost that she has had a commemorative stamp issued by Canada Post with her image on it. She is affectionately known as the phantom bride. According to the legend, a young couple was married in Banff around 1930, and after the wedding, the bride started to ascend the stairs to join her husband waiting at the top, only to trip on her gown. The gown brushed against some candles, catching fire. In the frantic melee that followed she tripped over her gowns long hem, falling down the stairs and breaking her neck. She has been seen ascending and descending the stairs as a transparent white spectre.

HAUNTED HOTELS:
TRANSITORY DANCES WITH THE DEAD

Stairs where the incident supposedly occurred. However, there seems to be no room for a candelabra, unless it was on the landing above right.

Obviously, the bride was subsequently denied her wedding night of conjugal bliss in the warm arms of her new husband, so there have also been those who have heard strange noises coming from the bridal suite. O.K., stop laughing, I know what you are thinking, but they are hearing those noises when the suite is empty.

Lynton Viñas

HAUNTED HOTELS:
TRANSITORY DANCES WITH THE DEAD

Edmonton, Alberta is a city that rises stark and bold on the plains as the great Canadian Via Rail train meanders its way toward the Rockies that tower in the distance. On the way to the resort town of Jasper, the train passes near the Hotel MacDonald. Sometimes, people board the train in Edmonton and as they dine in the evening enjoying one of the true great rail travel experiences left in North America, if they have stayed in the Hotel MacDonald, they often share their ghostly experiences in a hotel know to harbour several ghosts.

It appears that ghosts really like the eight floors in hotels, as many tales centre on the eighth floor in the MacDonald. However, sometimes it is not a human ghost, but an animal. Jesse James' dog could be heard barking at the St. James in Selma, Alabama, but the Hotel MacDonald can certainly top that. It seems that when they were building the hotel in 1914, one of the workman's horses just dropped dead. Although this happened on the ground floor, for some unknown reason, the horse can now, on occasion, be heard galloping up and down the eight floor hallway. On occasion, he does return to the ground floor, galloping about in the basement.

Apparently some other ghosts of the human type prefer the executive suites. Hey, if you are a ghost why not go first class? Guests in one suit have reported waking up to see a man sitting in a chair puffing away on a pipe. A few puffs though, and he, himself, puffs into oblivion.

HAUNTED HOTELS:
TRANSITORY DANCES WITH THE DEAD

Another spirit has materialized in a boatman's uniform, as the hotel used to attract some of the boat captains who plied the Saskatchewan River, which was a major fur trading route. These spirits usually appear on the fourth floor.

Not only have the guests seen spirits, but the staff report incidents of receiving phone calls from empty rooms ordering room service. They go up, unlock the unoccupied room and find the telephone off the hook.

Sometimes rooms will have the deadbolts used to lock the room from the inside. The only problem is there is no one in the room, so maintenance has to break the door down to get in. Although annoying, none of the ghosts seem ill-intentioned.

For many years there was a staff area used for breaks, and inside the lounge was an old switchboard that had been long ago disconnected. However, the switchboard would occasionally light up with rings from room 404. The staff would go up to room 404, and, it would be empty, but there on the nightstand would be a phone that was not connected to the switchboard off the hook. Other times, there would be strange music from the 1950's blaring out of the switchboard, despite the fact there was no radio in it. However, it was remembered that the hotel used to be the place where the Canadian Broadcasting Company broadcast from the top floor as it was the highest building in Edmonton and offered a great place for a tower so the signal could be transmitted free of interference.

HAUNTED HOTELS:
TRANSITORY DANCES WITH THE DEAD

When there are clouds overhead or especially a thunderstorm,
the Hotel MacDonald takes on an eerie appearance.

There is a hotel in St. Andrews, New Brunswick called the Algonquin which seems to be a favourite of ghosts. It is considered one of the most haunted places in the province. What is unusual is there were no odd accidental deaths during construction, and no guests dying under troubling circumstances. Still there appears to be many spirits who chose to linger here. Hey, it is a nice hotel, and spirits deserve a nice place, too.

HAUNTED HOTELS:
TRANSITORY DANCES WITH THE DEAD

There is an old cartoon series called *Casper the Friendly Ghost* and there is a ghost at the Algonquin, who may be just as friendly as Casper, because he is a bellhop who approaches guests and helps them in a variety of ways, only to disappear when the people turn away from him. This has been reported a number of times to the point were guests have left tips at the front desk for him, since he left before they could hand the tip to him. It would be interesting to see just what a ghost could do with money. As far as I know, the staff has not passed the tips on to him.

There is also a maid who apparently appears on occasion in the dining room. She only appears late at night, setting up the dining room for breakfast the next morning. Obviously, she was a night maid, and as a ghost still prefers the late evening shift.

A former night watchman jingles keys as he saunters up and down the hallways, unseen but heard. However, once when a guest was locked out of his room, the night watchman apparently materialized and let him in. When the man walked into the room, he turned around to tip the man and he had disappeared into thin air.

Crying is often heard coming from the bridal suite when it is empty. It is assumed to be a woman whose groom left her standing at the altar when he had a last minute change of heart. When guests are in the room, sometimes crying can be heard coming from the corners late at night.

There have been reports of electrical equipment going haywire in certain rooms on the third floor, and some guests have experienced apparitions in their rooms on this floor.

None of the ghosts at the Algonquin ever seem sinister. Apparently this place only attracts well-mannered spirits. The same cannot be said of the of the Fort Garry Hotel in Winnipeg Manitoba where a sinister figure in a dark Dracula-like cloak appears at the foot of the bed in room 202 smiling down at the occupants as blood drips from his eyes.

The Bessborough Hotel in the prairie town of Saskatoon, Saskatchewan had a devoted employee back in the 1920's who fell over a stair railing on the seventh floor, landing in the main lobby below to the shock of the guests. His ghost apparently carries grudge for his untimely demise and walks around in a grey uniform smiling at guests when he puts a fright into them.

The Hargrave Street Hotel in Winnipeg sat deserted in a residential area for years, but when it burned down in 2015 the spirits there apparently had no where to go, so they dispersed into

HAUNTED HOTELS:
TRANSITORY DANCES WITH THE DEAD

finding new places to haunt, as apparitions are often seen in vacant lots after dark. Before the hotel burned it had become known as Demon Hotel, and perhaps it was, as after its destruction by fire, beneath it were found dark, foreboding dungeon-like subterranean rooms that apparently had been hidden for years. What went on in those rooms?

Fort Garry Hotel →

Hargrave Street Hotel ↑
← *Bessborough Hotel*

Chapter 9

South African Scream That Shatters the Darkness

A Wadsworthian poem spoke of ghostly horror,
Grasping for that which shines eternity's light,
And here below this poem will earnestly borrow,
For this is a tale of ghostly demons and fright.

All hotels wherein men have lived and died
Are haunted in fact. Through the sullen doors
The dark phantoms on their errands glide,
With feet that make no sound upon the floors.

We meet them at the doorway, on the stair,
Along the passages they come and go,
Impalpable impressions on the air,
A sense of something moving to and fro.

Lynton Viñas   125

HAUNTED HOTELS:
TRANSITORY DANCES WITH THE DEAD

There are ghosts serving as dark hosts.
Uninvited they are. The illuminated hall
Is thronged with quiet offensive ghosts,
As silent as the pictures on the wall.

Some strangers at the fireside cannot see,
Nor hear the sounds others hear;
He but perceives what is; while unto me
All that has been is visible and clear.

We have no earthly claim to lands;
Owners and occupants of earlier dates
From graves forgotten stretch their dusty hands,
And sullenly cling to hotel estates.

The spirit-world around this land of sense
Floats like an atmosphere, and everywhere
Wafts through these earthly mists and vapours dense
A vital breath of more ethereal air.

Lynton Viñas

HAUNTED HOTELS:
TRANSITORY DANCES WITH THE DEAD

Our own lives are filled with poise

By opposite attractions and desire

The struggle of the instinct that enjoys

The noble pursuit for which we aspire.

These perturbations, this perpetual jar

Of earthly wants and aspirations high,

Come from the influence of an unseen star,

An entity unable to know he did die.

And as the moon from some dark gate of cloud

Throws o'er the sea a floating bridge of light

Across whose trembling planks our fancies crowd

Into the realm of mystery and night.

So from the world of spirits there descends

A bridge of darkness, connecting it with this,

O'er whose unsteady floor, that sways and bends,

Wander our thoughts above the dark abyss.

Here in hotels where others died

It is but a muffled scream heard

That makes us all know death lied

For the ghosts are being stirred.

One of my most exciting sojourns in South Africa was to the

Lynton Viñas 127

HAUNTED HOTELS:
TRANSITORY DANCES WITH THE DEAD

quaint little village of Simon's Town, where a colony of penguins frolics about the beach. Although that was the chief lure to this wonderful place that is about a one and one-half hour train ride paralleling the ocean from Cape Town, being a student at the time studying at the International Hotel School, I was also looking forward to spending my first night ever in a hotel which was rumoured to be haunted.

The Glen Lodge Hotel, also known as the Glencairn Hotel is over 100 years old. It is a structure that does not stand out majestically on the hillside in this little seaside community, but it blends in harmoniously with this little village that seems trapped in the 1950's or 1960's, peacefully embracing the new South Africa. This quaint little hotel is inviting, seeming to speak of laid back summer days in a hammock, enjoying the cool ocean breeze. Still, a horrible incident happened in room 6 here, which may have led to some restless spirits that now haunt it.

Lynton Viñas

HAUNTED HOTELS:
TRANSITORY DANCES WITH THE DEAD

The maid at the hotel, Renee Scott was the fiancé of the chef, but she rendezvoused with a man in room six for some afternoon delight. After the man left, she took her young son up to the room and as she was preparing him for a nap, the chef, having gotten word of what went on, in an enraged fury, walked in with a large butcher knife and proceeded to hack her to death while her son looked on in horror. After killing the woman, he picked up the boy and flung him down the stairs.

Many guests have claimed to see a dark-haired woman in a long white gown that appears in room mirrors, while others have seen a young boy running about in the kitchen. The boy apparently likes playing pranks by moving things around and breaking glasses. These are the two seemingly identifiable ghosts, but there appears to be three others that also frolic about on occasion. Fortunately, none of them seem malevolent, and thankfully there has never been a citing of the chef with butcher knife in hand.

Be sure to ask for room 6 if you stay here, and be polite and say hello to the dark haired woman in a long white gown if you pass her in the hallway. Unfortunately, she did not make an appearance while I was there.

HAUNTED HOTELS:
TRANSITORY DANCES WITH THE DEAD

Author Wayne Frye writes a book series featuring me as the main fictional character. Two of those books take place in the Karoo area of South Africa, and it is those two books I enjoy the most. One is entitled *Lynton, the Karoo Vampire and the Jewels of Omar Bin Abi*, and it mentions the town of Matjiesfontein several times as it is reputed to be the most haunted town in South Africa. There is a grand and great history of this small Karoo town, which is generally assumed to be the most haunted place in South Africa. Stories of ghost sightings abound, but none of the ghosts here seem to be particularly malevolent. Of course, some of those ghosts prefer the environs of a very comfortable hotel, and the Lord Milner Hotel has several ghosts that frolic about with no ill-intent.

Lucy is a translucent entity who floats around passages and stairs wearing – are you ready for this men – a sheer negligee. She was simply given the name Lucy by the current owners. There is no knowledge of whom she might be other than it is assumed she was someone who might have died long ago at the hotel. Additionally, voices can often be heard at night in empty rooms, and sometimes a loud argument can be heard with the crashes of plates and furniture, but when the room is opened, no one is there and all furnishings are in their proper place completely in tact.

Lucy is not the only ghost at the Lord Milner. There is a steep staircase on the second floor that leads to a door, and on that door is a plague reading, "Kate's Card Room." This leads to the room inside the central turret. On one side of the room is a locked door, wherein is a ladder to the roof.

At one time, this hotel was a hospital for British officers and also a rest resort for convalescents. It is not certain whether the ghost (named Kate) was a nurse for the officers' hospital or the convalescent home; nonetheless, as the story goes, she was a young woman named Kate who would play cards with the patients, but had an untimely death at 19. It appears that she loves to float about the hotel, having been seen in almost every area. Also, when guests go into the card room, shuffling cards can be heard as they often get the feeling that it is not just Kate there but others unseen who might resent the intrusion and then the door to the roof starts rattling. Some of the staff claims that while cleaning, they feel someone brush past them, look and see a ghost-like apparition that almost immediately dissipates.

HAUNTED HOTELS:
TRANSITORY DANCES WITH THE DEAD

There are a large number of haunted hotels in South Africa, but I will conclude with a few that illustrate the depth of hauntings in this wonderful country. Having called Cape Town my home for awhile, good ghost tales are just another grand part of the South African experience. It is a land that has known misery, bigotry, depravation, along with the horrors and evil of apartheid, only to emerge triumphant by embracing a harmonious magnanimous belief in the power of the human spirit to rise above the past and embrace hope for the future. Of course, ghosts know no politics, only the thrill of the haunt. So, let's take a look a few more examples of ghostly haunts in South Africa.

There are few places scarier than the Mountain Park Hotel in Bulwer, South Africa. It sets at the base of the Amahaqwa Mountains and was built in 1940. It is constructed in the Tudor style with dark wood beams and ceilings. Part of its charm is the somewhat crooked doors and the creaking floors.

The owners have grown accustomed to entities floating about the hotel. The third floor is seemingly the most haunted. So profound is the paranormal activity there they only rent rooms on that floor when they are fully booked as doors close by themselves, footsteps can be heard in the corridors, apparitions appear on stairways, and it is also common for entities to materialize in a translucent manner in the guests rooms only to immediately dissipate. It does seem that none of the ghosts are particularly malevolent, which is a positive.

Lynton Viñas

HAUNTED HOTELS:
TRANSITORY DANCES WITH THE DEAD

Downstairs in the bar and billiard room the owners say there are eight known spirits hovering about. One is assumed to be the original owner Mr. McMenigel, who went bankrupt before he finished building the hotel and committed suicide, no doubt, brought on by worries over his failing hotel.

Another ghost is as known as Mathilda, who can often be seen sitting on the staircase, chin in hands. Unhappy with the placement of her old school desk at the top of the stair landing, she will move it to a more suitable location on occasion.

A tall woman, called Ruth, who may have been Mathilda's governess and apparently fell from the third floor to her death, is particularly prone to wander about the entire hotel. There are those who claim that the Jacuzzi and sauna rooms are haunted by entities as sometimes the guests are overwhelmed with the feeling of a presence, even when they are alone.

A few guests have been frightened after seeing what they interpret as blood on the walls of their rooms, only to walk over and watch it dissipate. Although the most harrowing experiences occur on the third floor, many brave guests actually request accommodations there. Several television journalists and ghost investigators have indicated they sense the hairs on their necks bristling and are overwhelmed with the feeling of a presence.

And finally, there is a small white dog the owners have named Wisp, that has also been seen trotting merrily along the hallways on various occasions.

HAUNTED HOTELS:
TRANSITORY DANCES WITH THE DEAD

Anyone up for a night on the third floor
of the Mountain Park Hotel?

Near the town of Dargle, KwaZulu-Natal, South Africa is the Hebron Haven Hotel. Apparently, it is so beloved by past owners that they do not want to give it up even after death. One past owner, Carl Preller, settled in the Dargle area in 1849. It is rumoured that in order to keep his sons from squandering his fortune, he converted everything to gold coins, and those coins are buried somewhere on the grounds. There is apparently some credence to the rumour, as a box of coins was once unearthed. So, is there another one about the grounds just waiting to be discovered? Is that why Preller's ghost has been seen wandering about the grounds to make sure the other coins are not unearthed?

The current owner, Robert Pollabauer, recounts how he went to close the ladies' washroom window one night when he was locking up and had someone brush past me as he walked in. Only problem was there was no one there when he felt it.

On numerous occasions, guests have also spotted an old man sitting at the window in cabin two, looking out over the garden. The doors of empty cabins have been locked from within, and one female guest said her duvet was pulled off her and she was gently turned over from her stomach on to her back.

Where are those gold coins? Be careful if you look,
because old man Preller may be watching you.

Obviously, having been a Cape Town resident who embraces the nation of South Africa with great fondness is it little wonder that I am always looking for those special places that offer the unusual and unique in this magnificent country. South Africa has a long history of oppression from those who for too long embraced the abomination called apartheid, but today, the nation embraces ethnic and cultural diversity in the warm arms of hope that shines a beacon of light that even the ghosts of this lovely country, no doubt, welcome into their nether world in which all people can be equally frightened by things that go bump in the night and might just elicit that scream that shatters the darkness.

Chapter 10

Tangling with Ghosts

In the greenest Baguio valley
By graves of the long dead,
Once a fair hotel palace
Radiantly reared its head.

Banners yellow, glorious, golden,
On its roof did float and flow.
Yes, this hotel was a palace
So very, very long ago.

Ah, but abandoned now,
Within you feel the spirits
Flittering ghostly all about,
Whispering of death's merits.

Lynton Viñas

HAUNTED HOTELS:
TRANSITORY DANCES WITH THE DEAD

Evil things in robes of sorrow,

Assail this once high estate.

Ah, let us mourn, for now

This place is so desolate.

Gone is the former glory

That blushed and bloomed.

Is but a dim-remembered story

Of the old time entombed.

Here sullen ghosts dance forever,

Embracing the dark of death's door

From this lonely place to never dissever,

And haunt here evermore.

We all are travellers to death's door,

But still shiver when ghosts are seen

In the air and forlornly soar.

Look, look, look at the fiend!

(Lynton Viñas – © 2017)

Being Filipino by birth, perhaps it is obligatory that I include at least one haunted Filipino hotel in this book. Although the most famous haunted place in the Philippines is Balente Drive in Manila, there is a former hotel in the resort town of Baguio in northern Luzon, long abandoned that actually attracts overnight tourists in search of a frightful experience. I have been told stories as a child about the ghostly happenings here that would cause me many nights of restless sleep and nightmares.

The Philippines is a country deeply steeped in religion, because as a very poor nation, its citizens cling to the idea of an after-life where the streets are paved with gold and the first will be last and the last will be first. Their only hope is for an after-life that will ameliorate the economic misery of their current lives. So, is it any wonder that they embrace the idea of ghosts that linger in purgatory, waiting for that gate to the good-life to open, so they may enter eternity where there is no want, no denial of basic human dignity? One place where these ghosts wait in the darkness is the resort community of Baguio.

There is a place that was known as the Diplomat Hotel, but before it was a hotel, it had other lives. It began as a lavish vacation house for a wealthy Dominican order in 1910. It sets on a hill high above a valley, and when it was finished being remodelled in 1915, it was probably the most lavish place in all of Baguio, which is a bit of an anomaly, since the church represented by the Dominican order preaches humbleness and the embracing of Christ-like virtues of modest living. Nonetheless, they spared no expense making it as grandiose as possible.

During World War II there were many horrible and brutal deaths here as townspeople, fleeing the Japanese invasion, congregated on the hill, believing the Japanese would not bomb a religious sanctuary. The hundreds who died found out the Imperial Japanese Army had no qualms about bombing a religious sanctuary, just as the Americans had no qualms when the atomic bomb that was dropped on Hiroshima scored an almost direct hit on the only Catholic church in that city. The grotesque death of these people was particularly disconcerting as many victims languished in pain within the confines of the building for days with no medical aid before they mercifully died.

After the war, entrepreneurs bought the building and grounds for a very small amount of money and set out to rebuild. Finished in 1948, the Diplomat Hotel chain eventually bought it and converted it into a hotel. The hotel was managed by a Baguio-based charismatic spiritual healer named Tony Agpaoa who used unconventional means to cure people from a variety of ailments from cancer to warts. Since his death in 1987, the hotel ceased operation and was closed to the public. The rumours were that the hotel had trouble getting guests due to the constant howling heard from people apparently in intense pain. Assuming that Tony was not torturing people as part of his cures, which all evidence points to him not doing so, one might conclude that the tormented souls of those who suffered after the bombing might still be lingering about in spirit form.

Former Diplomat Hotel employees and guests claimed that they were in constant fear of strange sounds and headless apparitions that often appeared during the night inside the hotel. Since the Japanese beheaded many nuns and priests during the World War II, this may explain the headless nature of the rambling spooks.

Some years back, after it was closed to the public, local residents who lived nearby claimed that they could hear strange noises in the middle of the night. For instance, despite the fact that it didn't have doors, they could still hear banging doors, windows, clattering of dishes and voices of screaming people which seemed to be agonizingly real.

HAUNTED HOTELS:
TRANSITORY DANCES WITH THE DEAD

As you drive up the entrance, looking at the starkness, cold chills creep up and down your spine. Even the cross that still stands on the top of the building seems to be issuing an ominous warning that evil awaits inside. One visitor said that upon entering there is an instant chill and that a feeling of horror assaults the senses.

The Diplomat Hotel is said to pulsate with the energy of the dead even in the daylight, but the ghostly apparitions seem to prefer darkness. The gates to the place close at 5:00 PM, so the visitors are spared having to endure the screams and ghostly apparitions that prefer the night. The guards do not go inside after dark. Perhaps it is part of their contract, because the wages of guards in the Philippines are far too low to include tangling with ghosts!

HAUNTED HOTELS:
TRANSITORY DANCES WITH THE DEAD

Epilogue
Those Spectres That Haunt Us

Frostonian delight in poetry may shine.
As fluttering ghosts on souls want to dine
There is a journey to death we all take,
As the curtain of darkness we never shake.
Oh, but between life and death is a fine line.

They dwell in a lonely place I know
That vanished many a summer ago,
And left no trace but the cellar walls,
And a cellar in which the daylight falls,
And wild weeds now slowly grow.

O'er ruined fences the grape-vines shield
The woods come back to the mowing field;

Lynton Viñas 143

HAUNTED HOTELS:
TRANSITORY DANCES WITH THE DEAD

The orchard tree has grown one copse

Of wood where a woodpecker chops;

The footpath down to the well is healed.

I dwell with a strangely aching heart

In that vanished abode there far apart

On that disused and forgotten road

That has no dust-bath now for the toad.

Night comes; the black bats tumble and dart.

The whippoorwill is coming to shout

And hush and cluck and flutter about:

I hear him begin far enough away

Full many a time to say his say

Before he arrives to shout it out.

It is under the small, dim, summer star.

I know not who these mute folk are

Who share the unlit place with me.

Those stones out under the low-limbed tree

Doubtless bear names that the mosses mar.

They are tireless folk, but slow and sad,

Though two, close-keeping, are lass and lad.

With none among them that ever sings,

HAUNTED HOTELS:
TRANSITORY DANCES WITH THE DEAD

And yet, in view of how many things,

They are my companions as might be had.

In a place called Walden Pond, which is in Massachusetts, the great thinker Henry David Thoreau looked at life and said, "I have more lives to live." Are the ghosts looking for more lives to live? Are they unable to let go of that which they may have squandered. Far too many of us are trapped by life and not really living it. We need to better understand something else Thoreau said, "The mass of men lead lives of quiet desperation. What is called resignation is confirmed desperation. From the desperate city you go into the desperate country, and have to console yourself with the bravery of minks and muskrats. A stereotyped but unconscious despair is concealed even under what are called the games and amusements of mankind. There is no play in them, for this comes after work. But it is a characteristic of wisdom not to do desperate things."

What does the above have to do with haunted hotels? Simply that we must see beyond the dancing ghosts that apparently are clinging and longing for this thing called life. We all are waltzing in the ballroom of despair looking for meaning to life. Our exploration in the previous few pages of places where the dead return to haunt is more than a journey into the macabre, it is a stroll through the darkness that far too often engulfs us in fear – not fear of the dead, but fear of life. We are prone to forget what really counts in a world where too many people equate happiness to material things, especially since only a very small portion of people have garnered all the material things while the rest of us struggle to keep our heads above water. Life is, at best, a struggle in a world where work dominates our lives while we slave so that the few can benefit from the labour of the many. The ghosts that haunt the places described herein are but wayfarers on another plain of existence, lost in the search for the meaning to that which may well have no meaning. Ghosts are really nothing but manifestations of our own search for that which seems to always elude us in one way or another. Consequently, we must all search within ourselves and ask if those shadows that invade the darkness are really ghosts. Or are we the actual ghosts searching for a real life right alongside those spectres that haunt us?

HAUNTED HOTELS:
TRANSITORY DANCES WITH THE DEAD

Bibliography and References by Chapter

HAUNTED HOTELS:
TRANSITORY DANCES WITH THE DEAD

Chapter 1

National Park Service (2008-04-15). "National Register Information System". National Register of Historic Places. National Park Service.

"Rocky Mountain Legends". LegendsOfAmerica.com.

"Rocky Mountain National Park - Culture". US-Parks.com.

Turkewitz, Julie (3 September 2015). "Hotel That Inspired 'The Shining' Builds on Its Eerie Appeal". New York Times.

"The Stephen King Companion" Beahm, George Andrews McMeel press 1989

"Stephen King Country" Beahm, George Running Press 1999

Vvdailypress.com Archived October 18, 2006, at the Wayback Machine.

"Stephen King: America's Best Loved Boogeyman" Beahm, George Andrews McMeel Press 1998

"Stanley Hotel Ghost Story". Allstays.com.

"The Strange Occurrences at Stanley Hotel," Retrieved from: http://www.strangerdensions.com2016/04/25/stanley-hotel-haunted/

"Authentic Ghosts." Retrieved from: http://www.stanleyhotel.com/media-center/Stanley-Ghost-Stories-Shine-with-Authenticity

"Ghost Caught on Camera." Retrieved from: http://www.huffingtonpost.co.za/entry/stanley-hotel-ghost_us_57109ce1e4b0060ccda2e7f2

Chapter 2

"History of the Mermaid Inn". Mermaid Inn. Retrieved from: www.history of mermaidinn.com

"Ghost Stories from the Mermaid Inn Rye". Mermaid Inn Brochure . Retrieved 2017-01-03 from mermaidinn.com.

"The Mermaid Inn from Haunted Hotels". ghostbooks.net.

Chapter 3

la.curbed.com/2015/10/27/9907144/haunted-hotels-los-angeles

Body found in hotel water tank may be missing Canadian tourist. YahooNews, 20 February 2013.

Wallace-King, Donna (October 29, 2014). "True Tales of terror." KSLA News.

HAUNTED HOTELS:
TRANSITORY DANCES WITH THE DEAD

LAist.com: article by Juliet Bennett Rylah, 31 May 2016
http://therealdeal.com/la/2016/11/08/hotel-cecil-could-get-historical-cultural-status/
"James T. Bartlett, "Gourmet Ghosts 2: More Ghosts, Murders, Suicides and L.A. Weirdness", 2016. Research sourced from Los Angeles Times newspaper archives.
https://ladailymirror.com/2014/01/29/black-dahlia-and-the-cecil-hotel-another-good-story-ruined/
Duke, Alan (22 February 2013). "Hotel with corpse in water tank has notorious past". CNN.
Dean, Josh (Oct 27,2015). American Horror Story: The Cecil Hotel. Retrieved from: https://medium.com/matter/haunted-947d642a6d59#.y7v2ip1n1
Hamilton, Denise (2007-12-10). "Serial Killer Central - Native Intelligence". Laobserved.com.
"Body Found Inside Water Tank Atop Hotel Identified As Missing Canadian Tourist". CBS Los Angeles. February 19, 2013.
"We Thought the Water Tasted Funny."Daily Mail UK. February 20, 2013.
Melissa Pamer and Lolita Lopez (20 February 2013). "Body Found in Water Tank at Hotel is Missing Canadian Tourist: LAPD". NBC 4 Southern California.
William M. Welch (2013-06-21). "Elisa Lam's death ruled accidental". USA Today.
Nair, Drishya (June 21, 2013). Elisa Lam's Death. International Business Times.
Webb, Michael (December 1996). "Chateau Marmont Revisited". Architectural Digest.
Brown, Janelle. "The Chateau Marmont Is Ready for Its Close-Up". New York Times.
"Film locations for The Doors (1991)". LA TIMES.
"John Belushi, Manic Comic of TV and Films Dies.". New York Times.
"Frances Farmer Knocks Policeman Down", Los Angeles Times, January 15, 1943. Retrieved from LosAngeles Times Archives.

Chapter 4

"Hotel Galvez Ghosts." Retrieved from

HAUNTED HOTELS:
TRANSITORY DANCES WITH THE DEAD

http://www.galvestonghost.com/storiesgalvez.html
"St. Anthony Ghosts." Retrieved from:
https://omgrey.wordpress.com/2011/05/06/the-ghosts-of-st-anthony/
"Texas Ghosts." Retrieved from:
http://www.onlyinyourstate.com/texas/13-haunted-places-tx/
"Hotel Driskill Haunting." Retrieved from
https://www.hauntedrooms.com/product/driskill-hotel-haunted-ghost
National Park Service (2010-07-09). "National Register Information System". National Register of Historic Places. National Park Service.
"The Driskill" *Texas Historic Sites Atlas* Retrieved December 28, 2008.
Carmack, Liz. *Historic Hotels of Texas*, Texas A&M University Press: College Station, Texas, 2007. pp 76-80.
"The Driskill, a Historic Hotels of America member". Historic Hotels of America, 2014.
Williamson, Roxanne. *"DRISKILL HOTEL," Handbook of Texas Online".* Texas State Historical Association. Retrieved from: http://abclocal.go.com/ktrk/story?section=news/state&id=9021158
Stollznow, Karen. "Austin's Haunted Driskill Hotel," 21 May 2014. Retrieved from:
http://archive.randi.org/site/index.php/swift-blog/2373-austins-haunted-driskill-hotel.html

Chapter 5

"St. James Hotel One of Most Haunted." Retrieved on 12 January 2017 from:
http://blog.al.com/strangealabama/2012/04/selmas_st_james_hotel_one_of_t.html
"The Winecoff Hotel Fire." Atlanta Fire Department Commemorative Yearbook. Turner Publishing, Inc. p. 99.
"The Night of the Fire." Peachtree Burning. Glass Mountain Entertainment.
"The Crescent Ghosts" Retrieved from: http://www.haunted-places-to-go.com/crescent-hotel.html

HAUNTED HOTELS:
TRANSITORY DANCES WITH THE DEAD

"Myrtles Plantation". *National Park Service. Retrieved 24 March 2016.*

"Myrtles Plantation". *Myrtles Plantation.com.*

National Park Service "Explore the History and Culture of Southeastern Louisiana"

"Haunted Plantation - Myrtles Plantation Bed and Breakfast, St. Francisville, Louisiana" by Joe Nickell, *Skeptical Inquirer*, Septempter-October 2003.

"The Haunted Plantation". Mental Floss.

"Prairie Ghosts: Myrtles Plantation". *Retrieved from "Natchez Area Paranormal Society - Historical Archives".*

Kermeen, Frances. Myrtles Plantation, the True Story of Americas Most Haunted House.

Ghosts of Myrtles Plantation. HauntedRooms.com

Hawes, Jason; Wilson, Grant; Friedman, Michael Jan *(2007)*. *"The Myrtles February 2005." Ghost Hunting: True Stories of Unexplained Phenomena from The Atlantic Paranormal Society.* New York: Pocket Books. *pp. 135–147.*

Chapter 6

https://newengland.com/today/travel/new-england/things-to-do/best-haunted-hotels-and-inns-in-new-england/

Paradie, James. *Beal House Inn.* Retrieved from: http://scaredsheetlessncn.blogspot.co.za/2011/03/beal-house-inn.html

http://www.biography.com/news/the-lizzie-borden-house-haunted.

Lizzie Borden History. Wikepedia.com.

Orleans Waterfront Ghost Called Hannah Dances Naked. Retrieved from:
http://www.orleansinn.com/index.cfm?fuseaction=news.details&ArticleId=17&returnTo=ghost-stories

http://www.hawthornehotel.com/history/. Haunted Lodgings: Hawthorne Hotel - The Witching Hour. Retrieved from https://4girlsandaghost.wordpress.com/.../haunted-lodgings-hawthorne

Chapter 7

"Top Five Haunted Places." The Argentina Independent.

HAUNTED HOTELS:
TRANSITORY DANCES WITH THE DEAD

Retrieved from: www.argentinaindependent.com/life-style/ba/top-5-haunted-pla..
http://boredomtherapy.com/haunted-old-hotel/
Haunted Buenos Aires - Ghost Stories of the City – Retrieved on January 13, 2017 from:
wander-argentina.com/haunted-buenos-aires-ghost-stories
https://www.dazzling.news/a32/this-hotel-in-mexico-city-is-definitely-haunted
https://escritofederal.com/2015/12/09/la-posada-del-sol-the-decrepit-long-forgotten-but-newly-discovered-city-hotel/
http://www.mexconnect.com/articles/3863-mexico-city-legends-city-of-ghosts

Chapter 8
http://hammersonpeters.com/?p=964
http://www.edmontonsun.com/2015/07/03/100-years-of-hotel-macdonald-ghostly-residents
http://www.hauntedhovel.com/algonquinresort.html
http://travelsquire.com/canadas-haunted-hotels/

Chapter 9
http://www.news24.com/Video/SouthAfrica/News/watch-go-inside-one-of-sas-haunted-hotels-20160506
http://www.getaway.co.za/travel-ideas/places-to-stay/south-africas-haunted-hotels/
http://www.timeslive.co.za/sundaytimes/stnews/2016/08/28/In-search-of-rational-explanations-for-ghostly-happenings
http://www.news24.com/Archives/Witness/Spend-Halloween-at-one-of-these-KZN-haunted-hotels-if-you-dare-20150430
http://www.iol.co.za/travel/south-africa/kwazulu-natal/things-that-go-bump-in-the-night-1573201
www.holiday.org.za/mountainpark.html
www.hebronhavenhotel.co.za

Chapter 10
www.most-haunted-hotels-in-the-world/74259490/
https://en.wikipedia.org/wiki/Diplomat_Hotel